A COMPREHENSIVE GUIDE TO CRAFTING **PERFECT BREAD** AND **BEYOND**

# SOURDOUGH
## *Success*

MICHAEL CIACCO

SOURDOUGH SUCCESS
Copyright 2024 by Michael Ciacco
All rights reserved.

No portion of this book may be reproduced, copied, distributed, or adapted in any way, with the exception of certain activities permitted by applicable copyright laws, such as brief quotations in the context of a review or academic work. For permission to publish, distribute or otherwise reproduce this work, please contact the author.

ISBN paperback: 979-8-9911987-0-7
ISBN (eBook): 979-8-9911987-1-4

# CONTENTS

INTRODUCTION | WELCOME TO THE WORLD OF SOURDOUGH .................................................................. 1
INTRODUCTION | UNDERSTANDING THE MAGIC OF WILD YEAST. ............................................................ 2
INTRODUCTION | WHY SOURDOUGH? BENEFITS AND FLAVOR ................................................................ 3
GETTING STARTED | THE ESSENTIALS OF SOURDOUGH: TOOLS AND INGREDIENTS ............................... 5
GETTING STARTED | CREATING YOUR SOURDOUGH STARTER ................................................................. 7
GETTING STARTED | TROUBLESHOOTING: COMMON STARTER ISSUES ................................................... 9
CARING FOR YOUR STARTER | STORING YOUR STARTER. FRIDGE VS. COUNTER ................................... 11
UTILIZING DISCARD | THE ART OF DISCARD: WASTE NOT, WANT NOT .................................................. 13
THE BAKING PROCESS | UNDERSTANDING THE STAGES OF BAKING: AUTOLYSE AND BULK FERMENTATION ....... 15
THE BAKING PROCESS | SHAPING YOUR DOUGH: TECHNIQUES AND TIPS ............................................. 18
THE BAKING PROCESS | BAKING YOUR LOAF: OVEN SETUP AND STEAM ............................................... 21
TROUBLESHOOTING AND TIPS | COMMON BAKING ISSUES: SOLUTIONS AND FIXES ............................. 23
HELPFUL HINTS FOR HIGH ALTITUDE BAKING: TROUBLESHOOTING AND MAKING ADJUSTMENTS .......... 26
CONCLUSION ................................................................................................................................................ 28

**RECIPE SECTION** ........................................................................................................................................ 29

   **CLASSIC BREADS** ................................................................................................................................ 29
- CLASSIC SOURDOUGH BOULE .................................................................................................... 30
- WHOLE WHEAT SOURDOUGH ..................................................................................................... 32
- RYE SOURDOUGH ......................................................................................................................... 34
- SOURDOUGH BAGUETTES ........................................................................................................... 36
- SOURDOUGH FOCACCIA .............................................................................................................. 38

   **PASTRIES FOR BREAKFAST AND BRUNCH** ........................................................................................ 40
- SOURDOUGH CROISSANTS .......................................................................................................... 42
- SOURDOUGH CINNAMON ROLLS ................................................................................................ 43
- SOURDOUGH BLUEBERRY MUFFINS ............................................................................................ 44
- SOURDOUGH BANANA BREAD .................................................................................................... 45
- SOURDOUGH PANCAKES .............................................................................................................. 46
- SOURDOUGH WAFFLES ................................................................................................................ 47
- SOURDOUGH SCONES .................................................................................................................. 49
- SOURDOUGH STICKY BUNS ......................................................................................................... 51
- SOURDOUGH COFFEE CAKE ........................................................................................................ 52
- SOURDOUGH DANISH PASTRIES ................................................................................................. 53
- SOURDOUGH DONUTS ................................................................................................................. 55

## SOUTHERN .................................................................................................. 58
- SOURDOUGH CORNBREAD .......................................................... 60
- BUTTERMILK SOURDOUGH BISCUITS ............................................ 61
- SOURDOUGH HUSH PUPPIES ....................................................... 62
- SOURDOUGH JALAPENO CHEDDAR BREAD .................................. 63
- SOURDOUGH BISCUIT CINNAMON ROLLS .................................... 64
- SOURDOUGH FRIED CHICKEN ..................................................... 66
- SOURDOUGH SAUSAGE GRAVY ................................................... 67
- SOURDOUGH SWEET POTATO BISCUITS ...................................... 68
- SOURDOUGH PEACH COBBLER .................................................... 69
- SOURDOUGH PECAN PIE ............................................................. 71
- SOURDOUGH PIE CRUST ............................................................. 72

## ITALIAN INSPIRED ....................................................................................... 74
- SOURDOUGH FOCACCIA WITH ROSEMARY ................................. 76
- RUSTIC SOURDOUGH PIZZA WITH FRESHMOZZARELLA AND BASIL ... 77
- SOURDOUGH CIABATTA BREAD WITH SUNDRIED TOMATOES AND HERBS ... 78
- SOURDOUGH OLIVE BREAD WITH KALAMATA OLIVES AND THYME ... 79
- SOURDOUGH CAPRESE BREAD WITH CHERRY TOMATOES, MOZZARELLA, AND BASIL ... 80
- SOURDOUGH PARMESAN GARLIC BREADSTICKS ......................... 81
- SOURDOUGH PANETTONE WITH DRIED FRUIT AND NUTS ........... 82
- SOURDOUGH RISOTTO-STUFFED TOMATOES ............................. 83
- SOURDOUGH TIRAMISU WITH ESPRESSO AND MASCARPONE ..... 85
- SOURDOUGH CANNOLI WITH SWEET RICOTTA FILLING AND CHOCOLATE CHIPS ... 87

## MEDITERRANEAN INSPIRED ........................................................................ 90
- SOURDOUGH FOCACCIA WITH HERBS ........................................ 92
- SOURDOUGH GREEK FLATBREAD (PITA) ..................................... 93
- SOURDOUGH OLIVE BREAD ........................................................ 94
- SOURDOUGH MEDITERRANEAN PIZZA ....................................... 95
- SOURDOUGH SPANAKOPITA ....................................................... 96
- SOURDOUGH STUFFED GRAPE LEAVES ...................................... 98
- SOURDOUGH MEDITERRANEAN FLATBREAD (LAHMACUN) ........ 100
- SOURDOUGH OLIVE AND SUN-DRIED TOMATO BREAD .............. 102
- SOURDOUGH SUN-DRIED TOMATO AND BASIL BREAD .............. 103
- SOURDOUGH MEDITERRANEAN HERB FOUGASSE ..................... 104

## VEGETARIAN AND VEGAN ......................................................................... 106
- SOURDOUGH AVOCADO TOAST ................................................. 108
- SOURDOUGH VEGAN GARLIC BREAD ........................................ 109
- SOURDOUGH VEGAN PIZZA ....................................................... 110
- SOURDOUGH VEGAN BRUSCHETTA ........................................... 111
- SOURDOUGH VEGAN STUFFED MUSHROOMS ........................... 112
- SOURDOUGH VEGAN LENTIL SOUP WITH SOURDOUGH CROUTONS ... 113
- SOURDOUGH VEGAN SPINACH AND ARTICHOKE DIP ................ 114
- SOURDOUGH VEGAN FALAFEL ................................................... 115
- SOURDOUGH VEGAN ZUCCHINI BREAD .................................... 116
- SOURDOUGH VEGAN CHOCOLATE CAKE ................................... 118

## HEALTH-CONSCIOUS CREATIONS .......... 120
- SOURDOUGH MULTIGRAIN BREAD .......... 122
- SOURDOUGH CHIA SEED CRACKERS .......... 123
- SOURDOUGH SWEET POTATO PANCAKES .......... 124
- SOURDOUGH VEGAN LENTIL SOUP WITH SOURDOUGH CROUTONS .......... 125
- SOURDOUGH VEGGIE BUDDHA BOWL WITH TURMERIC TAHINI DRESSING .......... 127
- SOURDOUGH CHIA SEED PUDDING PARFAIT .......... 129
- SOURDOUGH SPINACH AND FETA STUFFED PORTOBELLO MUSHROOMS .......... 130

## ASIAN FUSION .......... 132
- SOURDOUGH KIMCHI PANCAKES .......... 134
- SOURDOUGH STEAMED BAO BUNS .......... 135
- SOURDOUGH SCALLION PANCAKES .......... 136
- SOURDOUGH VEGGIE SPRING ROLLS WITH PEANUT DIPPING SAUCE .......... 137
- SOURDOUGH TERIYAKI TOFU STIR-FRY .......... 139
- SOURDOUGH MATCHA SWIRL BREAD .......... 140
- SOURDOUGH COCONUT CURRY SOUP .......... 141
- SOURDOUGH CHAR SIU PORK BUNS .......... 142
- SOURDOUGH KOREAN BBQ BEEF TACOS .......... 144
- SOURDOUGH MANGO STICKY RICE .......... 146

## LATIN AMERICAN FLAVORS .......... 148
- SOURDOUGH AREPAS WITH AVOCADO SALSA .......... 150
- SOURDOUGH EMPANADAS FILLED WITH BEEF AND POTATOES .......... 151
- SOURDOUGH TOSTADAS WITH BLACK BEAN SALSA .......... 153
- SOURDOUGH PUPUSAS STUFFED WITH CHEESE AND BEANS .......... 155
- SOURDOUGH CHICKEN TORTILLA SOUP .......... 156
- SOURDOUGH PLANTAIN CHIPS WITH GUACAMOLE .......... 157
- SOURDOUGH CARNITAS TACOS WITH PINEAPPLE SALSA .......... 159
- SOURDOUGH ENCHILADAS WITH RED SAUCE .......... 161
- SOURDOUGH CHURROS WITH CHOCOLATE DIPPING SAUCE .......... 163

## HOLIDAY SPECIALS .......... 166
- SOURDOUGH CRANBERRY WALNUT BREAD .......... 168
- SOURDOUGH PUMPKIN SPICE BREAD .......... 169
- SOURDOUGH EGGNOG PANCAKES .......... 170
- SOURDOUGH GINGERBREAD COOKIES .......... 171
- SOURDOUGH STUFFING .......... 173
- SOURDOUGH HOLIDAY BREAD PUDDING .......... 174
- SOURDOUGH HOLIDAY WREATH BREAD .......... 175
- SOURDOUGH HOLIDAY STOLLEN .......... 177
- SOURDOUGH APPLE CIDER DONUTS .......... 179
- SOURDOUGH HOLIDAY BUCHE DE NOEL (YULE LOG) .......... 181

# INTRODUCTION
## Welcome to the World of Sourdough

Welcome to your sourdough journey! There truly is nothing better than a loaf of fresh bread. Making sourdough is a personal journey for everyone who has tried, made, and has the littlest bit of interest in learning sourdough making. For a lot of people, it's about having delicious fresh homemade bread. For others, it's a challenge they have to conquer.

Out of all the breads on this planet, sourdough is the most paradoxical of all. It's both simple and complex. A wonderful way to slow life down and it ends with a byproduct that can be a great source of pride, taking in that you just turned water and flour into something truly glorious.

Although it might seem intimidating, this book will break it down for you - step by step, crumb by crumb, leaving you with confidence when you're in front of dough, a banneton, a cast iron, and an oven. Here, we will explore sourdough's unique characteristics, process, endless possibilities, and the fulfilling joy it brings once served on the table.

# INTRODUCTION
## Understanding the Magic of Wild Yeast

Starter (or wild yeast) is the life force of your bread. It serves as the leavening of your sourdough. In essence, a starter is a mixture of flour and water (and time) that has been inoculated by yeast and bacteria. These yeast and bacteria are all around us and naturally occurring.

Wild yeast refers to a varied collection of one-celled beings that majorly come from the genus known as Saccharomyces. However, it's significant to note that there might be other species that might play a role in the existence of wild yeast. The strains of wild yeast aren't the same as the ones that are used for commercial yeast production, which are painstakingly established. They vary from place to place and, most of the time, it depends on factors like weather, the area's geography, and lastly, the eater's style of living.

This is the factor which makes sourdough distinct from other breads and what renders it unique. Employing naturally forming yeast and bacteria instead of commercial yeast, those creatures create the bread's natural leavening. Yeast excites gas, allowing the bread to expand, with lactic acid bacterium lending their characteristic sourness to the dough.

After you've established a starter, you'll find a whole ecosystem of microorganisms quietly working away in the flour and water. The bacteria known as Lactobacillus-sanfranciscensisoxidizes the carbohydrates in the flour, yielding the sugars on which the yeast can feed. One way to think of the carbs in the starter is as stored solar energy; with every turn of the molecular wheel, another of the sun's secret loops is captured in chemical form. These sugars, as any lover of the brewer's art knows, ferment. The primary fermenters are the yeasts Saccharomyces cerevisiae, for which one version of the joke is that all they do all day is eat sugar and fart, which is actually more or less true: The byproducts of their breathing are alcohol and carbon dioxide. Secondary fermenters, notably the bacteria that produce lactic acid, create a sourness at the same time they form a new substance, acetic acid. Then come the alcohols, the acids, and the esters, hundreds of which (at least) together create flavor. At some point the yeasts and bacteria run out of food and fall dormant. You have to wake them up (torture them a little) by feeding them.

# INTRODUCTION
## Why Sourdough? Benefits and Flavor

Sourdough is the anti-Wonderbread, requiring only two ingredients compared to Wonderbread's 20. Additionally, sourdough can take up to seven days to make from scratch, contrasting with the mere few hours required for commercial bread production. In 2020, sourdough-making gained popularity as a result of the worldwide lockdown, and people had more time on their hands. Even DIYers are in on the sourdough craze. Now, spending days baking bread is the cool thing to do. Instagram is full of DIY self-taught bakers making their own sourdough.

## Rediscovering Tradition

The first written record of sourdough dates back to around 4000 B.C. in ancient Egypt. The first written evidence of sourdough is from the pyramids, which contain hieroglyphs showing people making beer and bread.

The sourdough starter was discovered when a mixture of flour and water was left exposed. The mixture began to bubble and rise, a process we now know is called fermentation. Rather than throw out the odd-smelling and expanding mixture, the cook decided to bake it anyway.

The result? A large round, spongy loaf of bread that we now call sourdough. Since ancient Egypt, this method of bread making has been passed down from civilization to civilization, from ancient Rome to ancient Greece all the way to America. Using a sourdough starter was pretty much the only way of making bread for thousands of years.

But things started to change for sourdough during the latter half of the 19th century. As the population shifted towards cities and the need to feed people on a bigger scale arose, the creation of an industrialized bread system emerged. It wasn't until the mid-19th century that scientists caught on to the microbiology behind what makes bread rise. Once they knew about wild yeast and how it works, a race set off to figure out how to make it available to the masses.

## Nutritional Superiority

Sourdough is typically more nutritious than regular bread. It's easier to digest and a potentially better option for blood sugar control. What makes the sourdough starter so special are all the microorganisms derived from the fermentation process, which commercial bread misses out on. It uses an active dry yeast that simulates the chemical process that makes bread rise. However, it lacks the naturally occurring fungi and bacteria that sourdough bread has.

Here's why that matters: sourdough's slow fermentation process makes it a lot easier for our bodies to absorb important nutrients. All of those microorganisms in sourdough also promote gut metabolic health. Sourdough also doesn't lead to blood sugar spikes and crashes. It actually slows down the speed at which glucose is released into the bloodstream, which is a great thing for diabetics who have to watch their insulin levels.

Store-bought bread has also been put under intense scrutiny for the extra ingredients manufacturers add in order to extend shelf life. These include everything from extra gluten, fat, reducing agents, emulsifiers, enzymes, and preservatives.

# GETTING STARTED
## The Essentials of Sourdough: Tools and Ingredients

Making sourdough requires more practice in technique and method than a complex recipe. This means that the tools of the trade are straightforward, and the ingredients are something home bakers, even the most novice ones, already have in their pantry.

## Tools of the Trade

- **Digital Scale:** Accuracy is key in sourdough baking, so invest in a reliable digital scale to measure your ingredients precisely.

- **Mixing Bowls:** Have a selection of mixing bowls in various sizes for mixing your dough and performing different stages of the baking process.

- **Dough Scraper:** A dough scraper is invaluable for handling and shaping your dough, as well as cleaning your work surface.

- **Banneton or Proofing Basket:** These baskets are used to shape your dough during the final proofing stage, giving your loaves their characteristic shape and pattern.
- **Dutch Oven or Baking Stone:** A Dutch oven or baking stone helps create the perfect crust by providing even heat distribution and trapping steam during baking.
- **Lame or Razor Blade:** To score your loaves before baking, ensure they expand properly in the oven, and develop that signature artisanal look.
- **Kitchen Thermometer:** Essential for monitoring dough and oven temperatures accurately, especially during fermentation and baking.

## Key Ingredients

- **Flour:** The foundation of sourdough. Choose high-quality bread flour, whole wheat flour, or specialty flours for unique flavors and textures.
- **Water:** Use filtered or non-chlorinated water to avoid inhibiting the growth of beneficial bacteria in your starter.
- **Salt:** Enhances flavor and regulates fermentation, so be sure to use fine sea salt or kosher salt without additives.
- **Sourdough Starter:** The heart of your sourdough baking journey, this live culture of wild yeast and lactobacilli is what gives sourdough its characteristic tangy flavor and leavening power.
- **Optional Add-Ins:** Get creative with your sourdough by incorporating seeds, nuts, herbs, or dried fruits for added flavor and texture.

# GETTING STARTED
## Creating Your Sourdough Starter

By now, you should be familiar with what a starter is. It is a unique composition of wild yeast and bacterial organisms. They live everywhere: on fruits, on your skin, and on grains such as wheat, rye, emmer, pretty much everywhere.

Making a starter from scratch typically takes 7 days, depending on the type of flour and the environment you're in. Over time, your starter is going to become better at fermenting flour. That's why making sourdough bread is more challenging than plain yeast-based bread. However, it is also pretty simple when you have all the information.

Here's a step-by-step process that you can follow and serve as your guide for 7 days:

### Day 1: Mixing the Initial Starter

1. In your container, combine 100 grams (about 3/4 cup) of flour with 100 grams (about 1/2 cup) of water. Stir vigorously until well combined, ensuring no dry flour remains.
2. Cover the container loosely with a kitchen towel or lid, allowing airflow.
3. Let the mixture sit at room temperature (around 70-75°F or 21-24°C) for 24 hours.

### Day 2: Feeding the Starter

1. You may or may not see any signs of activity in your starter yet, and that's okay! It's still early in the fermentation process.
2. Discard half of the starter (about 100 grams) and add another 100 grams of flour and 100 grams of water to the remaining starter. Stir well to combine.
3. Cover and let the starter rest for another 24 hours.

### Days 3-7: Daily Feedings

1. By now, you should start to see some activity in your starter. It may begin to bubble and develop a slightly sour aroma.
2. Continue the daily feeding routine: Discard half of the starter and feed it with equal parts flour and water. Stir well and cover.

3. Repeat this process daily until your starter is consistently doubling in size within 6-8 hours after feeding and has a pleasant, tangy aroma. This may take anywhere from 5 to 7 days, depending on various factors such as temperature and flour type.

Around 12 hours after you feed your starter, you can check if your starter is ready. You can use the float test, where you scoop about half a teaspoon of the starter and drop it in a glass or bowl of water where it would ideally float. If it sinks, it's presumably not yet ready, so you should wait a couple more hours before baking.

There are also signs you should observe that tells you your starter is already at its peak:

- Your starter should be bubbly
- It should smell sour, similar to vinegar or yogurt
- Should double in size

If it didn't double in size, wait 12 hours and then proceed and feed it again just like you did before. If it's bubbly but the smell is too strong, it could be that you haven't achieved a good balance of yeast and bacteria; it could mean your balance is still off. If it's mild and subtle, and you can really smell that yogurt or vinegar, then you're ready. You're about to make your first bread dough. Congratulations!

# GETTING STARTED
## Troubleshooting: Common Starter Issues

With all the instructional materials available, it's normal to compare what you have at home to what is stated in the guide that you are following. It's very common to find differences and issues when it comes to growing a starter, especially if it's your first time doing it. Because it takes time to create it, seeing these roadblocks and inconveniences can be discouraging. Fortunately, these issues are more often than not salvageable, and there are usually ways to rectify them.

### Starter Not Rising

A starter not rising as expected is one of the most common concerns for new sourdough bakers. There are several factors why this happens and it's just a matter of you figuring out where it went wrong. Sometimes, these factors are out of your control, but easily resolvable.

**Temperature:** Yeast activity is dependent and sensitive to the temperature you are in. If you live in cooler areas or you have an air-conditioned kitchen, your start tends to rise slower. You can either wait a few more hours and see if there's more activity or keep your starter in a warmer environment. You can also invest in a proofing box or keep it in a cranked oven, but remember to check on it from time to time as it has a tendency to overflow.

**Feeding Schedule:** As mentioned earlier, you're on a bread schedule when baking sourdough. And this schedule starts as early as creating your starter. The key is feeding it at the same time each day. However, sometimes, the activity of the starter varies. If you see that it completes its rise and fall cycle within 12 hours, you want to try to use a lower inoculation, or, in other words, maintain less of your mature starter each day to try to slow down that rise and fall.

**Flour Type:** Different types of flour can affect the activity of your starter. Whole grain flour or flour with higher bran content tends to ferment slower than refined flour, causing slower activity. Rye flour has a lot of natural yeast and helps nourish your starter. Once your starter is active, the important thing to remember if you are using white flour is that you need to use unbleached flour because that bleaching process can get rid of a lot of the natural yeast and bacteria that live in the yeast and help your starter to thrive.

## Starter Smells Unpleasant

Remember, your starter should smell tangy or sour. However, it should never smell foul or unpleasant. These odors can range from smelling like acetone or vomit. This could indicate the presence of bacteria, or your starter may have been contaminated.

**Over Fermentation:** If you're feeding your starter too frequently or keeping it at warm temperatures, it may become over-fermented, leading to off flavors and odors. Try adjusting your feeding schedule and keeping your starter in a slightly cooler environment.

**Contamination:** Other than the foul odor, you can also spot if your starter has been contaminated by mold or other unwanted bacteria. If you see something fuzzy or pink/orange streaks on the edges of the jar or the starter itself, it most probably is mold. This can happen if the equipment you use when stirring the starter isn't cleaned properly or the jar is left open and something has gotten in to contaminate it. Unfortunately, when this happens, you will have to throw your starter and start over.

If your starter smells unpleasant, it's important to address the issue promptly to prevent further problems. Pay close attention to any changes in odor or appearance and take appropriate action to remedy the situation.

## Starter Separates or Forms Hooch

A common problem that happens to everyone is a hooch. It's a gray liquid that you can occasionally see forming at the top of your starter. This happens when you neglect your starter and fail to feed it for a long period of time. However, it's nothing scary at all.

**Stir Before Feeding:** One reason a hooch might develop is because the flour isn't hydrated enough during feeding. All you have to do is make sure that you thoroughly stir the water and flour when feeding. You may use a tiny spatula to make sure you are able to access the curve at the bottom of your jar when dry flour usually stays.

**Adjust Feeding Ratio:** If you have been consistent with feeding, hooch might indicate that you need to provide more food for your yeast and bacteria. Try adding more water and flour (in equal parts) and observe the activity of your starter. Once you have achieved the right activity and have not seen the development of the hooch, take note of that ratio and use it as a standard when feeding.

# CARING FOR YOUR STARTER
## Storing Your Starter: Fridge vs. Counter

Once you've successfully cultivated your sourdough starter, the next step is deciding how to store it. You can store the starter on the countertop at room temperature or in the refrigerator. Both methods are perfectly acceptable, depending on how often you bake.

### Storing on the Countertop

If you're frequently baking sourdough, like in bakeries where you have to produce bread every day, storing it on the countertop is a more popular choice. However, there are factors you need to consider.

**Active Fermentation:** When stored at room temperature, your starter remains active and ready to use at a moment's notice. Because of this, you have to keep an eye out on your starter to make sure it's not over-fermenting, especially in the hotter seasons.

**Consistent Feeding:** To maintain the health of your starter on the countertop, you have to remember to feed it consistently—about once a day or every 12 hours, depending on how hot or cool your kitchen is. This consistent feeding routine helps keep the yeast culture thriving and ensures an active starter for baking.

**Quick Availability:** With your starter readily accessible on the countertop, there's no need for pre-planning. When you store a starter in the refrigerator, you'd have to bring it to room temperature anyway before using it. This is why storing on the countertop is ideal for bakeries – to cut the time of waiting for the starter to achieve its desired temperature.

**Temperature Considerations:** Room temperature can vary depending on your kitchen environment. Ideally, your kitchen should be between 70-75°F (21-24°C) for optimal fermentation. But no worries if yours runs hotter and cooler, as you can easily gauge what your starter needs through observation. If your kitchen tends to be cooler or warmer, you may need to adjust your feeding schedule accordingly.

## Storing in the Refrigerator

Home bakers store their starters in the refrigerator. This way, the maintenance isn't as demanding because the starter tends to slow down. They would only need to feed the starter every once a week. Here's what you need to know about storing your starter in the fridge:

**Slowed Fermentation:** Low temperature significantly slows the fermentation process. This frees your time, allowing you to feed your starter less frequently. The yeast activity decreases when you refrigerate your starter, which also helps preserve it for longer periods. Some starters even last for years.

**Extended Feeding Intervals:** Depending on your starter's activity, you can feed your starter once a week or even fortnightly. This schedule is also dependent on how much you bake. Either way, this flexibility offers you a break from sourdough and baking in general.

**Conserving Flour:** Refrigeration reduces the amount of flour needed to feed your starter since the fermentation process is slowed down. This can be beneficial if you want to minimize flour usage or if the availability of flour is a concern in your area.

**Reviving Your Starter:** Before using a refrigerated starter in a recipe, it's important to revive it by leaving it on the counter until room temperature and feeding it again. Through this process, you are basically waking the yeast up again and returning to its active state.

## Choosing the Right Storage Method

Deciding whether to store your starter on the countertop or in the fridge is entirely up to you, as well as your baking habits, schedule, and preferences. But to make things simple, if you are a home baker wanting to bake artisan bread occasionally, store it in the fridge. On the other hand, if you're a bakery owner producing bread on a daily basis, a countertop will be the better option for you.

What you need to remember is to be consistent and attentive to what your sourdough needs. As mentioned in the previous chapter, it's very much like owning a pet which you have to observe to maintain its health. As for any living organism, every starter is different in terms of activity and its needs. It can take a bit of time to get used to your starter schedule but once you get to know it, soon you and your starter will be at a similar pace.

# UTILIZING DISCARD
## The Art of Discard: Waste Not, Want Not

Now that you have a starter, you know full well the amount of excess that you have to throw away. Well, the good news is you don't necessarily have to throw them. This excess is better known as discard, which is very versatile as it gives the signature tangy flavor you can find in sourdough bread. Seasoned bakers carry various recipes and projects with them that use discard. In addition, you can give these discards away to friends who are interested in making their own starter.

To make the most of the discard, you must first appreciate its composition so you can envision what you can do with it. As it's directly from the starter, even if it's not at its peak, the discard is still rich in flavor and microbial activity, which adds to its tangy profile. However, this does not limit you to sour end-products only. You can still use the discard for a variety of recipes ranging from savory to sweet.

Utilizing discard benefits the baker in two ways: reducing food waste and eliminating the feeling of guilt when throwing it out; and in addition, it gives bakers, especially beginners, to experiment with wild yeast. It's a good venue for trial and error since as in theory, if you're consistent, you pretty much have another discard to play around with every week.

With the amount of discard in your hand and the knowledge of its versatility, you can now explore more recipes that can benefit from the discard's flavor and composition. Here are easy popular recipes that you can try in your kitchen.

- **Sourdough Pancakes:** Everything you want in a pancake is here – light and fluffy. What makes these pancakes special is the distinctive sourdough tang that is added to the classic pancake flavor profile. Simply combine discard with flour, eggs, milk, and a touch of sweetness to create a batter that transforms into golden orbs of deliciousness on the griddle.

- **Sourdough Waffles:** If you're a waffle person rather than a pancake person, waffles can also be made with discard. It will come out crisp on the outside and tender on the inside. Mix the discard with flour, baking powder, eggs, and butter to create a batter that yields waffles with a delightful tang and satisfying texture.

- **Sourdough Banana Bread:** Step up your banana bread by incorporating sourdough discard into the batter. The tangy notes of the discard complement the sweetness of ripe bananas, resulting in a moist and flavorful loaf that's perfect for any time of day.

- **Sourdough Pizza Dough:** For more savory and dinner options, you can also transform your discard into a crusty pizza dough with a slight hint of sourness that can highlight your tomato sauce. Combine discard with flour, water, yeast, and salt to create a dough that's perfect for crafting homemade pizzas topped with your favorite ingredients.

- **Sourdough Crackers:** The simplest recipe for a discard might be crackers. They are crisp, crunchy, full of flavor, and pair perfectly with cheese, dips, or enjoyed on their own. Perfect for grazing tables or for snacking. Utilize discard to create a dough that's rolled thin, baked until golden brown, and seasoned to perfection.

# THE BAKING PROCESS
## Understanding the Stages of Baking: Autolyse and Bulk Fermentation

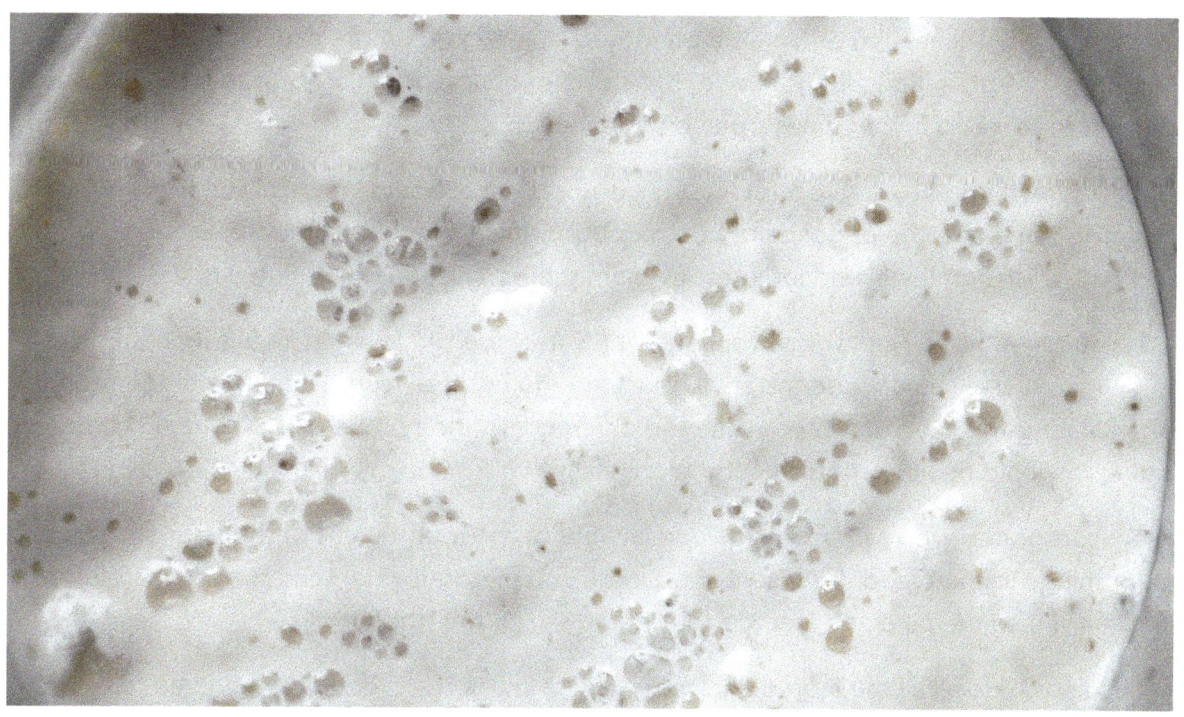

Having an active starter is just the beginning. Now we get to the nitty-gritty. You are now ready to bake your sourdough bread.

Begin by weighing your flour. In sourdough baking, we use a formula called baker's percentage, where the amount of flour is always equal to 100%; and every other ingredient is a percentage of that flour. For example, a dough with 80% hydration means that 80% of the total weight of the flour is what you add in water.

Baker's percentage:
100% flour
20% starter
2% salt

The amount of water is all up to how high the hydration you want for the dough.

## Autolyse: A Moment of Rest and Transformation

Autolyse is an initial step in bread making. This is a process in which water and flour are gently mixed together and set to rest for a period of time before mixing continues. This helps the gluten to form and hydration to begin. If starter is the life force of your bread, gluten is the backbone

Typically, autolyse is done without a starter. At this stage, you only want to hydrate the flour and make sure there are no dry areas. You don't have to mix it thoroughly; only work the water through using your hand or a bench scraper. To ensure you have no dry spots, you can pinch the dough with your hands while turning it and getting the dry flour that may be trapped at the bottom of the bowl.

Sometimes, you will have to add a little bit more water to the dough, especially when you are using whole-grain flour. If this happens, we recommend adding 5g of water at a time and making sure you adjust your baker's percentage.

Mix until everything is hydrated without any dry spots. You should end up with a gnarly-looking dough that is the opposite of bread dough, which should be smooth on the surface. Cover with a kitchen towel and let it rest at room temperature for 30 minutes to 2 hours.

When you're ready, you can weigh your starter (20% of the total weight of the flour) and add it to your autolyse. You can use the same pinching method to incorporate the starter into the dough. During this process, you can see the difference in the texture of the flour and water mixture. It should now be stretchier and more elastic.

Once incorporated, you can now add your salt (2% of the total weight of the flour). Salt does a lot of things to the bread. It seasons the bread, and also helps tighten up all of the gluten. You can also use the pinching method to add the salt to the dough.

You have now added all the ingredients you need to make the bread. It's now time to work the dough a little bit before proceeding to bulk fermentation. You can do this using the stretch and fold method.

Picture the dough in four quadrants. Scoop and grab the upper left quadrant, lifting it up and folding it towards the center, kind of folding it to itself. Then, turn the bowl a little bit to the left and do the same stretching and folding process.

Continue this motion until you see a couple of things: increased smoothness or a more uniform texture, less stickiness due to the absorption of water, increased elasticity where the dough springs back to its shape, and extensibility. Usually, you would have to work the dough for 10-15 minutes. Cover and let the dough rest for an hour.

## Bulk Fermentation: Nurturing the Dough to Life

The principal process of sourdough making is the bulk fermentations. Bulk because we will work the full amount of dough at once, and fermentation because this is the stage where the yeast in the starter is feeding on all of the new food sources and produces gas.

Once you come back to the dough after letting it rest for an hour, you'll notice that the surface has settled for a bit and appears flat. This means that your dough has relaxed from the work you did earlier. We want to maintain all of the gluten that it has developed. Some of that gluten relaxes and can start to break down if you let it.

To counteract that, we can do a series of folds as it goes through bulk fermentation. These folds help continue to build and also maintain the strength in the dough. The folding action helps the gluten strands to link up and form long chains that you often see on bread doughs.

To do the folds for bulk fermentation, dampen your hands and grab the dough from the opposite sides of the bowl, lifting it, stretching it upward, and folding the dough onto itself. Give the bowl a 90° turn and repeat the process. Remember to be gentle and try your best avoiding to deflate the gasses that you are currently building up.

Cover the dough again and let it rest. After an hour, repeat the same folding process. Do it two more times.

# THE BAKING PROCESS
## Shaping Your Dough: Techniques and Tips

We are now ready to move on to the next stage of the process which is forming, shaping and setting the loaf up for proofing.

### Understanding Dough Consistency

After bulk fermentation, you should be able to see the transformation of your dough. It should almost double in volume and it jiggles when you give the bowl a slight shake. This is an indication that you are done with the bulk fermentation and ready to proceed with the next step.

### Preparing Your Work Surface

Dust the surface with a little bit of flour. Any flour will do. However, using rice flour does a better job in protecting the basket liners because it results in less sticking as it does not absorb water the way what flour does.

## Pre-Shape and Bench Rest

Pre-shaping is a step that allows the dough to get into a more organized form. Place the dough on your bench, which is the surface you will be working onto, by tipping the bowl and sort of letting the dough pull itself out of it. Do this very carefully and try not to pop the air bubbles that were developed. Start by gathering one edge of the dough and folding it to the center, then working your way around the dough. This is typically 6 times until it's round in shape. Once you get to that shape, flip it over (seam side down) to a non-floured surface, cup it in your hands and drag around your counter in a small circle, maximizing the surface tension so that you'll end up with a tighter dough.

After pre-shaping, allow the dough to rest on the bench for a short period, typically around 20-30 minutes. This bench rest relaxes the gluten, making the dough easier to shape and reducing the risk of tearing.

## Shaping Techniques

There are various shaping techniques you can use depending on the type of loaf you're making and personal preference. Here are some common techniques:

1. **Boule (Round Loaf):** To shape a boule, gently stretch the edges of the dough towards the center, rotating the dough as you go to create tension. Once you've formed a tight ball, flip it seam side down and use your hands to shape it into a smooth round.

2. **Batard (Oblong Loaf):** For a batard, start by gently flattening the dough into a rectangle. Fold the top third of the dough towards the center, then fold the bottom third over the top. Use your hands to seal the seam along the length of the dough, then roll it slightly to elongate and tighten the loaf.

3. **Baguette:** To shape a baguette, start by gently pressing the dough into a rectangle. Fold one long edge of the dough towards the center, then fold the opposite long edge over the top. Use your hands to seal the seam, then gently roll the dough into a long cylinder, tapering the ends slightly.

## Final Proofing

Proofing is like the second rise that occurs after the loaf has been shaped. With bulk fermentation, you are developing the gas and the air in the loaf. With proofing, it's all about developing flavor. It's a chance for the dough to relax a little bit for the lactic acid to work more.

Proof the loaf for 60-90 minutes. Some indicators to tell when your loaf is proofed are when the dough is settled more into their baskets, if they're a little bit domed, expansion in size and when they pass the poke test.

Poke test is when you poke a finger through the dough and it should spring back slowly and leave a little indentation which is a sign that the gluten has relaxed.

Once it's proofed, cover and leave in the fridge overnight. The next day will be your bake day.

## Scoring the Dough

The reason we slash the bread is so that we give the dough a predictable place where it can start to expand. Without scoring, the brea will still rise. However, it would crack and fissure at random places.

There are a lot of scoring methods you can use. Experienced bakers use this as a creative outlet by using intricate and artful designs. For beginners, a simple individual lengthwise slash is advisable.

# BAKING YOUR LOAF
*Oven Setup and Steam*

## Oven Setup

An important step in bread baking is preheating your oven thoroughly. This ensures proper heat distribution before you put your dough in.

Bread bakes ideally at a super high temperature. A common recommendation is to preheat to typically around 450-500°F
(232-260°C).

## Steam Injection

Dutch oven bread baking is a really common method. It's the easiest and most effective method for home bakers when baking bread. With Dutch ovens, you are baking in a closed vessel for part of the time with a very tight fitting lid that builds up steam as the dough begins to bake. The point is to keep the starches in the dough pliable so that in the early part of baking when it's really hot and the lid is on, you're going to create moisture that will then turn into steam.

All the gas that's trapped in the dough is going to heat up and expand the dough, creating the holes in your bread. The steam will help the bread to achieve that maximum expansion called the oven spring. Towards the end of baking, you take the lid off and let the dry heat of the oven create a beautiful golden brown crust.

Before baking, you'd also want to preheat your Dutch oven or whatever vessel you're using for the bread.

## Baking Techniques

Once your oven is preheated, it's time to load your dough into the hot Dutch oven. Grab a piece of parchment paper and make sure its width is the same as the length of the dough and allow plenty extra (6+ inches) to use as handles. Put it on top of the banneton and gently turn the bread over and slowly lift off the basket. This is where you score your dough.

Bring out your Dutch oven and grab the sides of the parchment paper to lift the loaf. Place it inside, cover with lid, and bring it back into the oven, working carefully but quickly so that the heat won't dissipate.

The dough will bake at 300° with the lid on for 20-30 minutes, then remove the lid and bake for an additional 30 minutes.

## Monitoring and Troubleshooting

After taking the lid off, you'll eventually smell a toasty, savory, almost caramelly flavor. It will also develop a deep brown color, but not burnt.

In the event you notice an uneven browning throughout the process, especially at the top of the dome, you can cover that part of the loaf with an aluminum foil. This can prevent over-darkening on the top and allows for the bread to have an even color.

## Cooling and Savoring the Fruits of Your Labor

To take the load out of the Dutch oven, you can use tongs or a heatproof spatula. Use the parchment paper overhang to slightly lift the bread, grab it with your chosen tool, and place on a wire rack to cool completely.

It's important to let the bread cool before slicing as it's still continuing to bake for a few more hours. This also allows the crust to be more crisp and the crumb to fully develop. Once you feel that the bottom of the loaf is completely cool to the touch, that is your go signal to slice the bread.

# TROUBLESHOOTING AND TIPS
## Common Baking Issues: Solutions and Fixes

As with any other project, the process of sourdough baking cannot alway be seamless, especially when you are dealing with days of hard work and complex techniques. These challenges often have an easy and readily available solution, as these issues are very common even to the most experienced bakers.

### 1. Dough Too Sticky or Wet

When handing the dough, one of the most frustrating issues you can come across is how sticky and wet the dough can be. This makes it harder for it to be handled and shaped. There are a lot of factors why this happens but most of the time, it is due to the type of flour and the hydration level.

**Solution:** Adjusting Hydration and Flour

The default solution to a sticky dough is adding flour. However, adding too much can affect the texture of the bread and can leave you with pockets of dry flour if not handled properly. It is better to flour the surface or your hands first and see if it makes a difference. If not, add a small amount of flour gradually. For beginners, it is also advisable to use lower levels of hydration for easier handling.

## 2. Dense or Flat Loaves

Breads that have not domed, flat, dense, and lacking in volume are also common. It is still edible, but it loses all the other qualities that people love in a bread which is a good crumb. This issue is due to insufficient fermentation, improper shaping, or inadequate gluten development.

**Solution:** Proper Fermentation and Shaping

To address dense or flat loaves, be attentive during the fermentation process. You can follow the guides written on a recipe to the T, but every kitchen is different. It is better to look for indicators of fermentation rather than depending on estimated time. Once you gauge the time needed by the dough, set it as your standard when making the next batches of bread in the same kitchen. Another way to correct this is by practicing proper shaping techniques and being gentle during this process to avoid popping air bubbles.

## 3. Uneven Oven Spring

Uneven and irregular-shaped loaf can be frustrating after all the hours you spent preparing the dough. An uneven oven spring can look like a lopsided dome, a curve coming out of random areas, or a tear to the side even if you did not score it.

**Solution:** Even Heat Distribution and Scoring

To create a good oven spring, make that your oven is properly preheated and that heat is evenly distributed throughout. Some ovens might hit a hot spot especially for older ones. To counter this, you can use a baking stone or cast iron skillet for better heat retention and distribution. Proper scoring of the dough before baking is also important. Scoring allows steam to escape and prevents excessive expansion in specific areas.

## 4. Sourdough Bread Too Sour or Not Sour Enough

A sourdough's signature flavor lies in its tanginess. However, there could be times where the bread is too sour to the point of it being jarring when eaten, while others prefer a more pronounced tang.

**Solution:** Adjusting Fermentation Time and Temperature

## 5. Overly Dark or Burnt Crust

A common frustration for bakers is ending up with loaves that have overly dark or burnt crusts. This affects the overall appearance of the bread and gives out a bitter taste. Your oven might be hitting a warm spot or not calibrated properly.

**Solution:** Monitoring Oven Temperature and Bake Time

Monitor your oven temperatures accurately. An oven thermometer can be a perfect tool for the job. However, it's not unusual for the thermometers built into ovens to be slightly off, and sometimes they need to be reset. It's sometimes difficult to gauge temperature issues during the baking process and adjust, so I recommend sticking with a plan and then adjusting the next batch if needed. Browning the top crust of bread is definitely an area where intervention is helpful. If the top crust is browned before the rest of the loaf can catch up, you can shield the dark part by tenting aluminum over it.

# HELPFUL HINTS FOR HIGH ALTITUDE BAKING
## *Troubleshooting and Making Adjustments*

Baking sourdough at high altitudes presents a distinct difficulty. Decreased atmospheric pressure and the drier air have a profound impact on yeast activity, fermentation, and the entire baking process.

At elevated altitudes, reduced air pressure impacts various elements of the sourdough baking process:

- **Yeast Activity:** The increased fermentation and the time needed for the dough to rise is faster due to yeast. If the dough is not thoroughly monitored, over proofing can result.

- **Evaporation of Water:** Due to the arid atmosphere found at elevated elevations, water evaporates rapidly. This can lead to bread drying out. A higher level of water in the bread dough makes the dough more workable and is a key factor in preventing a dry end product.

- **Temperature Variations:** Temperature is often erratic and can vary more in higher locations. Because of this, the dough demands careful attention and monitoring during the fermentation and proofing stages.

To mitigate the difficulties of baking at high altitudes, it is advisable to make the following modifications:

- **Starter reduction:** To decrease the amount of starter in your sourdough recipe and reduce fermentation with the goal of preventing over fermentation. Start by reducing the yeast in your formula by 10 to 25 percent and fine-tune that amount based on the dough's performance. This means that your standard baker's percentage will change.

- **Increase Liquid:** Though dealing with sticky dough is tricky in any kitchen, in a high altitude, stickiness can help keep bread from drying out. Shoot for a higher-than-average hydration to offset the amount of evaporation that takes place.

- **Longer Fermentation:** Extending fermentation allows the dough to more fully develop its flavors, helping it to balance the faster rising caused by diminished air pressure.

- **Lower Oven Temperature:** Drop the baking temperature by 25°F (14°C) to keep the crust from becoming crispy too quickly and from becoming excessively brown.

- **Utilize a Dutch Oven:** Employing a lidded Dutch oven to bake sourdough bread captures steam which results in a moist environment. Dutch ovens also provide increased influence over the ambient conditions and temperature, especially beneficial when baking at high altitudes where moisture disappears so abruptly.

Baking at higher elevations can often be an unpredictable endeavor, and it may take a few tries to figure out the necessary modifications needed for your location and conditions. It might help to keep a notes app and record your process, so that you can refer back to it, if changes need to be made you can reference them later. Use this information to refine your techniques and achieve consistent results.

Hydration level, fermentation, and the ambient temperature are some of the factors that require a special attention when baking at high altitude. These variables can affect your process and the overall outcome of your bread. Recipes that are readily available are usually not suitable for these types of locations. However, when you familiarize yourself with these factors, you can be able to easily adjust and gain better control of the entire breadmaking process.

# CONCLUSION

You can easily go to the shops and local artisan bakeries and easily get yourself a loaf of bread. Sourdough bread making is a long process, and while it requires simple tools and ingredients, people that jump on this journey should have the dedication it needs to be able to see the beautiful golden brown end-result.

On the other hand, there are also people who find it meditative due to its slow and methodical process. It is almost an escape to the pace of society which is continuing to be faster, and the attention span we develop is getting shorter and shorter. There is something about making a complex product out of your own hand using things that are available in your kitchen. Fulfilling is another word that comes up when bakers slice into their loaves.

Now that you know the basics of making sourdough bread, there are no limits on what you can explore and create. Have fun playing around with techniques, tools, and flavors in your home kitchen.

May your crust always be crisp and your crumb alway be open!

RECIPE SECTION
CLASSIC BREADS

# CLASSIC SOURDOUGH BOULE

In the world of sourdough baking, few things are as iconic and satisfying as a perfectly baked boule. The word "boule" comes from the French word for "ball," and indeed, this round loaf with its signature crust and soft, airy crumb is a delight to behold and devour. Now we shall delve into the art and science of crafting the quintessential Classic Sourdough Boule.

**PREP TIME:** 6 hours (including mixing, autolyse, bulk fermentation, shaping, and proofing)
**COOK TIME:** 45 minutes | **YIELD:** 1 boule (about 12 servings)

### INGREDIENTS:

- 400g bread flour
- 100g whole wheat flour
- 350g active sourdough starter (100% hydration)
- 320g water
- 10g salt

### CALORIES: 150 PER SERVING

Total Fat: 1g
Saturated Fat: 0.5g
Cholesterol: 0mg
Sodium: 250mg
Total Carbohydrate: 30g
Dietary Fiber: 2g
Sugars: 0g
Protein: 5g

### INSTRUCTIONS:

1. **Mixing:** Begin by weighing out your flours and combining them in a large mixing bowl. Add the water and sourdough starter to the flours, stirring gently with a dough whisk or wooden spoon until just combined. Cover the bowl with a kitchen towel or plastic wrap and let it rest for 30 minutes. This initial rest, known as the autolyze, allows the flour to fully hydrate and the gluten to begin developing.

2. **Adding Salt:** After the autolyse, sprinkle the salt evenly over the dough. Use your hands or a dough scraper to incorporate the salt into the dough thoroughly. Remember, salt not only adds flavor but also helps to regulate fermentation.

3. **Bulk Fermentation:** Now, it's time for the bulk fermentation phase. Over the next 3 to 4 hours, perform a series of stretches and folds every 30 minutes. To do this, wet your hands slightly, then grab one side of the dough, stretch it up, and fold it over the center. Repeat this process for each side of the dough, rotating the bowl as needed. These folds help strengthen the dough's structure and redistribute yeast and fermentation byproducts.

4. **Shaping:** Once the dough has completed bulk fermentation, it's ready to be shaped into a boule. Gently transfer the dough to a lightly floured work surface. With lightly floured hands, shape the dough into a tight round by folding the edges into the center, creating tension on the surface. You can use a bench scraper to help shape the dough if needed.

5. **Proofing:** Place the shaped boule into a floured proofing basket or a bowl lined with a floured kitchen towel, seam side up. Cover the dough loosely with plastic wrap or a damp cloth and let it proof at room temperature for 1 to 2 hours, or until it has increased in size by about 30-50%. To test if it's ready, gently press your finger into the dough. If the indentation slowly springs back, it's proofed and ready for baking.

6. **Preparing the Oven:** About 30 minutes before the dough has finished proofing, preheat your oven to 450°F (230°C). Place a Dutch oven or baking cloche into the oven as it preheats. This will help create a steamy environment for optimal crust development.

7. **Baking:** Once the oven is preheated and the dough is fully proofed, carefully remove the hot Dutch oven or cloche from the oven. Carefully transfer the boule into the preheated vessel, seam side down. Score the top of the dough with a sharp knife or lame to allow for expansion during baking. Cover the Dutch oven or cloche with its lid and place it back into the oven.

8. **Final Bake:** Bake the boule covered for 20 minutes to trap steam and encourage oven spring. After 20 minutes, remove the lid and continue baking for an additional 20-25 minutes, or until the crust is deeply golden brown and the loaf sounds hollow when tapped on the bottom.

9. **Cooling and Enjoying:** Once baked, remove the boule from the oven and transfer it to a wire rack to cool completely. Allow the loaf to cool for at least 1 hour before slicing into it. This resting period allows the crumb to set properly and ensures the best texture and flavor. Then, slice into your beautiful Classic Sourdough Boule, savoring the aroma, the crusty exterior, and the soft, tangy crumb with each bite.

**TIPS:**

- Experiment with different flours and hydration levels to customize the flavor and texture of your boule.
- Don't rush the fermentation process. Properly developed dough leads to better flavor and structure.
- If you don't have a proofing basket, you can proof the boule seam side down on a parchment-lined baking sheet.
- For added flavor, consider incorporating seeds, herbs, or other mix-ins into your dough during mixing.
- Practice makes perfect! Don't be discouraged if your first few loaves don't turn out exactly as you hoped. With time and practice, you'll master the art of baking the perfect boule.

With these detailed instructions and helpful tips, you're well on your way to creating your own masterpiece: a Classic Sourdough Boule that's as beautiful as it is delicious. Happy baking!

# WHOLE WHEAT SOURDOUGH

There's a rustic charm to whole wheat sourdough that speaks of tradition and wholesomeness. This hearty loaf boasts a depth of flavor and a satisfying texture that sets it apart from its white flour counterparts. In this recipe, we'll delve into the nuances of crafting a delicious whole-wheat sourdough loaf that's sure to become a staple in your baking repertoire.

**PREP TIME:** 7 hours (including mixing, autolyse, bulk fermentation, shaping, and proofing)
**COOK TIME:** 45-50 minutes | **YIELD:** 1 large loaf (about 12 servings)

### INGREDIENTS:

- 400g whole wheat flour
- 100g bread flour (for added gluten strength)
- 350g active sourdough starter (100% hydration)
- 320g water (adjust as needed based on flour absorption)
- 10g salt

### CALORIES: 140 PER SERVING

Total Fat: 1.5g
Saturated Fat: 0.5g
Cholesterol: 0mg
Sodium: 220mg
Total Carbohydrate: 25g
Dietary Fiber: 3g
Sugars: 1g
Protein: 4g

### INSTRUCTIONS:

1. Preparing the Dough:
   - In a large mixing bowl, combine the whole wheat flour and bread flour.
   - Add the active sourdough starter to the bowl, followed by the water.
   - Using a dough scraper or your hands, mix the ingredients until they come together to form a shaggy dough. Avoid over-mixing at this stage.

- Cover the bowl with a kitchen towel or plastic wrap and let the dough rest for 30 minutes. This resting period, known as autolyse, allows the flour to fully hydrate and the gluten to start developing.

2. Incorporating the Salt:
   - After the autolyse, sprinkle the salt evenly over the surface of the dough.
   - Using wet hands or a dough scraper, gently incorporate the salt into the dough by folding and pressing it in. Be careful not to deflate the dough too much.

3. Bulk Fermentation:
   - Cover the bowl again and let the dough undergo bulk fermentation at room temperature (ideally around 75°F or 24°C) for about 4-6 hours. During this time, perform a series of stretch and folds every 30 minutes for the first 2 hours. This helps strengthen the gluten and improve the dough's structure.

4. Shaping the Loaf:
   - Once the dough has completed bulk fermentation and has increased in volume by about 30-50%, it's time to shape the loaf.
   - Lightly flour your work surface and gently transfer the dough onto it.
   - Divide the dough in half if making two smaller loaves or leave it whole for a larger loaf.
   - Shape the dough into a round or oval shape, depending on your preference, using a gentle folding and shaping technique.

5. Cold Fermentation:
   - Place the shaped dough onto a well-floured proofing basket or a lined bowl, seam side up.
   - Cover the dough with a kitchen towel or plastic wrap and transfer it to the refrigerator for cold fermentation. Let it rest overnight or for at least 8-12 hours. This slow fermentation process enhances the flavor and texture of the bread.

6. Baking the Loaf:
   - Preheat your oven to 450°F (230°C) with a Dutch oven or baking stone inside for at least 30 minutes.
   - Once adequately preheated, carefully remove the dough from the refrigerator and transfer it to a piece of parchment paper.
   - Score the top of the dough with a sharp knife or bread lame to allow for controlled expansion during baking.
   - Using the parchment paper as a sling, carefully place the dough into the preheated Dutch oven or onto the baking stone.
   - Bake covered for 20-25 minutes, then uncover and bake for an additional 20-25 minutes or until the crust is deep golden brown and the loaf sounds hollow when tapped on the bottom.
   - Once baked, transfer the loaf to a wire rack to cool completely before slicing. Resist the temptation to cut into it too soon to allow the crumb to set properly.

Enjoy the wholesome aroma and robust flavor of your freshly baked whole wheat sourdough. Whether enjoyed toasted with a smear of butter or used as the foundation for your favorite sandwiches, this bread is sure to delight your taste buds and nourish your body and soul.

# RYE SOURDOUGH

Rye sourdough bread holds a special place in the hearts of many sourdough enthusiasts. Its distinct flavor, hearty texture, and rich aroma make it a favorite choice for those seeking a more robust and earthy loaf. In this recipe, we'll dive into the art of crafting the perfect rye sourdough, exploring techniques, tips, and a step-by-step recipe to guide you through the process.

**EXPLORING RYE FLOUR**

Rye flour, derived from the rye grain, offers a unique flavor profile and nutritional benefits that set it apart from traditional wheat flour. With its lower gluten content and higher levels of fiber and nutrients, rye flour adds depth and complexity to sourdough bread. When combined with a sourdough starter, rye flour undergoes a fermentation process that enhances its flavors, resulting in a loaf with a delightful tanginess and robust character.

**PREP TIME:** 7.5 hours (including mixing, autolyse, bulk fermentation, shaping, and proofing)
**COOK TIME:** 45-50 minutes
**YIELD:** 1 loaf (about 12 servings)

## INGREDIENTS

Before we begin our rye sourdough journey, let's gather the ingredients needed for this recipe:

- 300g bread flour
- 200g dark rye flour
- 350g water (at room temperature)
- 100g active sourdough starter (100% hydration)
- 8g salt

## CALORIES: 130 PER SERVING

Total Fat: 1g
Saturated Fat: 0.5g
Cholesterol: 0mg
Sodium: 260mg
Total Carbohydrate: 25g
Dietary Fiber: 2g
Sugars: 0g
Protein: 4g

## INSTRUCTIONS

1. Mixing the Dough
   - In a large mixing bowl, combine the bread flour, dark rye flour, and water. Use a dough whisk or your hands to mix the ingredients until a shaggy dough forms.
   - Cover the bowl with a kitchen towel or plastic wrap and let it rest for 30 minutes. This resting period, known as autolyse, allows the flour to hydrate fully and develop gluten.

2. Incorporating the Starter and Salt
   - After the autolyse period, add the active sourdough starter to the dough. Use your hands or a dough scraper to incorporate the starter thoroughly.
   - Sprinkle the salt over the dough and continue to mix until well combined. The dough will become smoother and more elastic as the gluten develops.

3. Bulk Fermentation
   - Cover the bowl again and let the dough undergo bulk fermentation at room temperature for about 4-6 hours. During this time, perform a series of stretch-and-folds every 30 minutes for the first 2 hours to strengthen the dough.

4. Shaping and Final Proof
   - Once the dough has doubled in size and shows good fermentation activity, it's time to shape it. Gently pre-shape the dough into a round or oval shape and let it rest on the counter for 20-30 minutes.
   - After the resting period, shape the dough into its final form and place it into a well-floured proofing basket, seam side up.
   - Cover the basket with a kitchen towel or plastic wrap and refrigerate the dough for an overnight cold proof, typically 12-16 hours.

5. Baking the Loaf
   - Preheat your oven to 450°F (230°C) with a Dutch oven or baking stone inside. Once the oven is hot, carefully transfer the cold dough into the preheated Dutch oven or onto the baking stone.
   - Score the top of the dough with a sharp knife or razor blade to allow for expansion during baking.
   - Bake the loaf covered for 20 minutes, then remove the lid or cover and continue baking for an additional 20-25 minutes, or until the crust is golden brown and the internal temperature reaches about 200°F (93°C).
   - Once baked, remove the bread from the oven and let it cool on a wire rack for at least an hour before slicing and serving.

## ENJOYING YOUR RYE SOURDOUGH

Congratulations! You've successfully baked a delicious loaf of rye sourdough bread. The crust should be crisp, and the crumb dense yet tender, with a delightful tanginess imparted by the sourdough starter. Whether enjoyed plain, with a smear of butter, or alongside your favorite soup or stew, this rye sourdough is sure to delight your taste buds and satisfy your soul. Happy baking!

# SOURDOUGH BAGUETTES

Ah, the classic French baguette - with its crispy crust and airy crumb, it's a staple in bakeries worldwide. And what better way to enjoy this beloved bread than by making it yourself with your own sourdough starter? In this recipe, we'll dive into the art of crafting sourdough baguettes, from mixing the dough to achieving that perfect golden bake.

**PREP TIME:** 7 hours (including mixing, autolyse, bulk fermentation, shaping, and proofing)
**COOK TIME:** 20-25 minutes | **YIELD:** 3-4 baguettes (about 12 servings)

**INGREDIENTS:**

- 400g bread flour
- 300g sourdough starter (100% hydration)
- 240g water
- 8g salt

**CALORIES: 160 PER SERVING**

Total Fat: 1.5g
Saturated Fat: 0.5g
Cholesterol: 0mg
Sodium: 300mg
Total Carbohydrate: 30g
Dietary Fiber: 1g
Sugars: 0g
Protein: 4g

**INSTRUCTIONS:**

1. Preparing the Dough:
    - In a large mixing bowl, combine the bread flour and water, stirring until a shaggy dough forms. Cover the bowl with a kitchen towel and let it rest for 30 minutes. This resting period, known as autolyse, allows the flour to hydrate fully and develop gluten.
2. Incorporating the Starter:

- After the autolysis, add the sourdough starter to the dough mixture. Using your hands or a dough scraper, gently fold the starter into the dough until evenly incorporated. Sprinkle the salt over the dough and continue to fold until the salt is fully integrated.

3. Bulk Fermentation:
    - Cover the bowl with plastic wrap or a damp kitchen towel and let the dough undergo bulk fermentation at room temperature (around 70°F or 21°C) for 4 to 6 hours. During this time, the dough will rise and develop flavor as the wild yeast in the starter works its magic.

4. Shaping the Baguettes:
    - Once the bulk fermentation is complete, lightly flour a work surface and turn the dough out onto it. Divide the dough into equal portions, depending on how many baguettes you wish to make. Working with one portion at a time, gently shape the dough into a rectangle, then fold the sides towards the center and roll it up tightly, sealing the seam.

5. Final Proofing:
    - Place the shaped baguettes onto a floured couche or parchment-lined baking sheet, leaving enough space between them to expand. Cover them loosely with plastic wrap or a damp towel and allow them to proof at room temperature for 1 to 2 hours, or until they have increased in size by about 50%.

6. Preheat the Oven:
    - About 30 minutes before baking, preheat your oven to 450°F (230°C). If you have a baking stone or steel, place it in the oven to preheat as well. You may also prepare a steam pan by placing it on the bottom rack of the oven.

7. Scoring and Baking:
    - Just before baking, use a sharp knife or a bread lame to score the tops of the baguettes with diagonal slashes. This not only adds an aesthetic touch but also helps the bread expand properly in the oven. Transfer the baguettes to the preheated oven and bake for 20 to 25 minutes, or until they are golden brown and have a hollow sound when tapped on the bottom.

8. Cooling and Enjoyment:
    - Once baked, remove the baguettes from the oven and let them cool on a wire rack for at least 30 minutes before slicing into them. While it may be tempting to dig in immediately, allowing the bread to cool ensures that the crumb sets properly and prevents it from becoming gummy. Serve your freshly baked sourdough baguettes with butter, cheese, or your favorite toppings, and savor the fruits of your labor.

**TIPS AND VARIATIONS:**
- For added flavor, consider incorporating herbs, seeds, or olives into the dough during the mixing stage.
- Experiment with different scoring patterns to create unique designs on your baguettes.
- If you prefer a softer crust, you can brush the baguettes with water before baking or cover them with a damp cloth during cooling.
- With practice and patience, you'll soon be baking up delicious sourdough baguettes that rival those from your favorite bakery. So roll up your sleeves, dust off your apron, and let's get baking!

# SOURDOUGH FOCACCIA

Focaccia, with its golden crust, airy crumb, and infused olive oil flavors, is a beloved Italian bread that's perfect for showcasing the tangy goodness of sourdough. In this section, we'll delve into the delightful world of sourdough focaccia, exploring its versatile nature and providing you with a step-by-step recipe to create your own flavorful masterpiece.

### INTRODUCTION TO SOURDOUGH FOCACCIA

Focaccia originates from Italy, particularly from the Liguria region, where it's been cherished for centuries as a versatile and delicious bread. Traditionally, focaccia is made with a simple dough of flour, water, yeast, salt, and olive oil. However, by incorporating sourdough starter into the mix, we elevate the flavor profile and texture, resulting in a bread that's richer, more complex, and utterly irresistible.

**PREP TIME:** 7-10 hours (including mixing, first rise, second rise, and optional overnight fermentation)
**COOK TIME:** 20-25 minutes | **YIELD:** 1 focaccia (about 8 servings)

### INGREDIENTS

To make sourdough focaccia, you'll need the following ingredients:
- 300g all-purpose flour
- 200g sourdough starter (at 100% hydration)
- 200g warm water
- 30g olive oil (plus extra for drizzling)
- 8g salt
- Toppings of your choice: rosemary, olives, cherry tomatoes, sea salt, etc.

### CALORIES: 180 PER SERVING

Total Fat: 2g
Saturated Fat: 1g
Cholesterol: 5mg
Sodium: 350mg
Total Carbohydrate: 35g
Dietary Fiber: 2g
Sugars: 1g
Protein: 5g

## INSTRUCTIONS

1. **Prepare the Dough:** In a large mixing bowl, combine the sourdough starter, warm water, and olive oil. Mix well until the starter is fully dissolved in the water.

2. **Incorporate the Flour and Salt:** Gradually add the all-purpose flour and salt to the bowl, stirring with a wooden spoon or your hands until a shaggy dough forms.

3. **Knead the Dough:** Transfer the dough to a clean, lightly floured surface. Knead the dough for about 5-7 minutes until it becomes smooth, elastic, and slightly tacky.

4. **First Rise:** Place the dough in a lightly oiled bowl, cover it with a kitchen towel or plastic wrap, and let it rise at room temperature for 4-6 hours, or until doubled in size. Alternatively, you can let it rise in the refrigerator overnight for a longer fermentation and enhanced flavor.

5. **Prepare the Pan:** Drizzle a generous amount of olive oil into a baking pan or sheet tray, spreading it evenly to coat the entire surface.

6. **Shape the Dough:** Once the dough has risen, gently transfer it to the prepared pan. Using your fingertips, press and stretch the dough to evenly fill the pan, creating dimples as you go.

7. **Second Rise:** Cover the pan with a kitchen towel or plastic wrap and let the dough rise again for 1-2 hours at room temperature, or until it puffs up slightly.

8. **Add Toppings:** Preheat your oven to 425°F (220°C). Before baking, dimple the dough once more with your fingertips. Then, sprinkle your desired toppings over the surface of the dough, pressing them in lightly.

9. **Bake the Focaccia:** Place the pan in the preheated oven and bake for 20-25 minutes, or until the focaccia is golden brown and sounds hollow when tapped on the bottom.

10. **Finish and Serve:** Once baked, remove the focaccia from the oven and drizzle with additional olive oil, if desired. Let it cool slightly before slicing and serving. Enjoy your homemade sourdough focaccia as a delightful snack, accompaniment to meals, or as the star of your next gathering.

# SOURDOUGH **PASTRIES**
## FOR BREAKFAST AND BRUNCH

Sourdough starter isn't just for bread; it can elevate your breakfast and brunch game to new heights with a variety of delicious pastries. From flaky croissants to sweet cinnamon rolls, these sourdough-based treats are sure to become family favorites. Get ready to impress your loved ones with these ten mouthwatering recipes!

1. [Sourdough Croissants](#)
2. [Sourdough Cinnamon Rolls](#)
3. [Sourdough Blueberry Muffins](#)
4. [Sourdough Banana Bread](#)
5. [Sourdough Pancakes](#)
6. [Sourdough Waffles](#)
7. [Sourdough Scones](#)
8. [Sourdough Sticky Buns](#)
9. [Sourdough Coffee Cake](#)
10. [Sourdough Danish Pastries](#)
11. [Sourdough Donuts](#)

# SOURDOUGH CROISSANTS

**PREP TIME:** 8-12 hours (including dough preparation, folding, chilling, and rising time)
**COOK TIME:** 15-20 minutes | **YIELD:** 12 croissants

## INGREDIENTS:

- 1 cup active sourdough starter
- 2 cups all-purpose flour
- 2 tablespoons sugar
- 1 teaspoon salt
- 1 cup unsalted butter, cold

## CALORIES: 250 PER SERVING

Total Fat: 15g
Saturated Fat: 10g
Cholesterol: 50mg
Sodium: 180mg
Total Carbohydrate: 25g
Dietary Fiber: 1g
Sugars: 5g
Protein: 4g

## INSTRUCTIONS:

1. In a large mixing bowl, combine the sourdough starter, flour, sugar, and salt. Knead until a smooth dough forms.
2. Roll the dough into a rectangle about 1/4 inch thick.
3. Cut the cold butter into thin slices and arrange them over two-thirds of the dough.
4. Fold the unbuttered third over the buttered middle third, then fold the remaining third over the top.
5. Roll out the dough again into a rectangle and repeat the folding process two more times, chilling the dough in the refrigerator for 30 minutes between each fold.
6. After the final fold, roll out the dough and cut it into triangles. Roll each triangle from the base to the tip to form croissants.
7. Place the croissants on a baking sheet lined with parchment paper, cover them with a towel, and let them rise at room temperature for 2-3 hours.
8. Preheat the oven to 375°F (190°C). Brush the croissants with egg wash and bake for 15-20 minutes, or until golden brown.

# SOURDOUGH CINNAMON ROLLS

**PREP TIME:** 10-12 hours (including dough preparation, rising time, and final proofing)
**COOK TIME:** 25-30 minutes | **YIELD:** 12 rolls

## INGREDIENTS:

- 1 cup active sourdough starter
- 3 cups all-purpose flour
- 1 cup warm milk
- 1/4 cup melted butter
- 1/4 cup sugar
- 1 teaspoon salt
- 1 tablespoon ground cinnamon
- 1/2 cup brown sugar
- Cream cheese frosting (optional)

## CALORIES: APPROXIMATELY 280 PER SERVING

Total Fat: Approximately 8g
Saturated Fat: Approximately 5g
Cholesterol: Approximately 20mg
Sodium: Approximately 260mg
Total Carbohydrate: Approximately 48g
Dietary Fiber: Approximately 1g
Sugars: Approximately 20g
Protein: Approximately 5g

## INSTRUCTIONS:

1. In a large mixing bowl, combine the sourdough starter, flour, warm milk, melted butter, sugar, and salt. Knead until a smooth dough forms.
2. Cover the bowl with a towel and let the dough rise at room temperature for 8-12 hours or overnight.
3. After the dough has risen, punch it down and roll it out into a rectangle about 1/4 inch thick.
4. Spread the melted butter over the dough, then sprinkle the cinnamon and brown sugar evenly on top.
5. Roll up the dough tightly from the long side and slice it into rolls about 1 inch thick.
6. Place the rolls in a greased baking dish, cover them with a towel, and let them rise at room temperature for 1-2 hours.
7. Preheat the oven to 375°F (190°C). Bake the cinnamon rolls for 25-30 minutes, or until golden brown.
8. Allow the rolls to cool slightly before drizzling them with cream cheese frosting, if desired.

Sourdough Pastries

# SOURDOUGH BLUEBERRY MUFFINS

**PREP TIME:** 15 minutes | **COOK TIME:** 25-30 minutes | **YIELD:** 12 rolls

## INGREDIENTS:

- 1 cup active sourdough starter
- 2 cups all-purpose flour
- 1/2 cup sugar
- 1/2 cup milk
- 1/4 cup melted butter
- 1 egg
- 1 teaspoon vanilla extract
- 1 teaspoon baking powder
- 1/2 teaspoon baking soda
- 1/4 teaspoon salt
- 1 cup fresh or frozen blueberries

## CALORIES: 180 PER SERVING

Total Fat: 6g
Saturated Fat: 3.5g
Cholesterol: 30mg
Sodium: 200mg
Total Carbohydrate: 30g
Dietary Fiber: 1g
Sugars: 12g
Protein: 3g

## INSTRUCTIONS:

1. Preheat the oven to 375°F (190°C). Line a muffin tin with paper liners or grease the wells with butter.
2. In a large mixing bowl, combine the sourdough starter, flour, sugar, milk, melted butter, egg, and vanilla extract. Mix until just combined.
3. Add the baking powder, baking soda, and salt to the bowl, and gently fold them into the batter.
4. Gently fold the blueberries into the batter until evenly distributed.
5. Divide the batter evenly among the muffin cups, filling each about two-thirds full.
6. Bake the muffins for 20-25 minutes, or until a toothpick inserted into the center comes out clean.
7. Allow the muffins to cool in the pan for 5 minutes before transferring them to a wire rack to cool completely.

# SOURDOUGH BANANA BREAD

**PREP TIME:** 15 minutes | **COOK TIME:** 60-70 minutes | **YIELD:** 1 loaf (about 10 servings)

## INGREDIENTS:

- 1 cup active sourdough starter
- 1 1/2 cups mashed ripe bananas (about 3 bananas)
- 1/2 cup melted butter
- 1/2 cup sugar
- 2 eggs
- 1 teaspoon vanilla extract
- 1 3/4 cups all-purpose flour
- 1 teaspoon baking soda
- 1/2 teaspoon salt
- 1/2 cup chopped nuts (optional)

## CALORIES: 200 PER SERVING

Total Fat: 7g
Saturated Fat: 4g
Cholesterol: 35mg
Sodium: 220mg
Total Carbohydrate: 30g
Dietary Fiber: 2g
Sugars: 15g
Protein: 4g

## INSTRUCTIONS:

1. Preheat the oven to 350°F (175°C). Grease a 9x5-inch loaf pan.
2. In a large mixing bowl, combine the sourdough starter, mashed bananas, melted butter, sugar, eggs, and vanilla extract. Mix until well combined.
3. Add the flour, baking soda, and salt to the bowl, and mix until just combined.
4. If using nuts, fold them into the batter until evenly distributed.
5. Pour the batter into the prepared loaf pan and spread it out evenly.
6. Bake the banana bread for 60-70 minutes, or until a toothpick inserted into the center comes out clean.
7. Allow the bread to cool in the pan for 10 minutes before transferring it to a wire rack to cool completely.

## SOURDOUGH **PANCAKES**

**PREP TIME:** 5 minutes | **COOK TIME:** 10 minutes | **YIELD:** approximately 8-10 pancakes

### INGREDIENTS:

- 1 cup active sourdough starter
- 1 cup all-purpose flour
- 1 cup milk
- 1 egg
- 2 tablespoons melted butter
- 2 tablespoons sugar
- 1 teaspoon baking soda
- 1/2 teaspoon salt
- Butter or oil for cooking

### CALORIES: 180 PER SERVING

Total Fat: 6g
Saturated Fat: 3.5g
Cholesterol: 40mg
Sodium: 250mg
Total Carbohydrate: 25g
Dietary Fiber: 1g
Sugars: 5g
Protein: 4g

### INSTRUCTIONS:

1. In a large mixing bowl, combine the sourdough starter, flour, milk, egg, melted butter, and sugar. Mix until well combined.
2. Add the baking soda and salt to the bowl, and mix until just combined.
3. Heat a griddle or large skillet over medium heat and lightly grease it with butter or oil.
4. Pour the pancake batter onto the hot griddle, using about 1/4 cup of batter for each pancake.
5. Cook the pancakes for 2-3 minutes on one side, or until bubbles form on the surface.
6. Flip the pancakes and cook for an additional 1-2 minutes, or until golden brown on both sides.
7. Serve the pancakes hot with your favorite toppings, such as maple syrup, fruit, or whipped cream.

# SOURDOUGH WAFFLES

**PREP TIME:** 15 minutes | **COOK TIME:** 3-5 minutes per waffle | **YIELD:** 4-6 waffles

### INGREDIENTS:

- 1 cup active sourdough starter
- 1 cup all-purpose flour
- 1/2 cup milk (preferably whole milk)
- 2 tablespoons melted butter or neutral oil (such as vegetable or canola oil)
- 1 large egg
- 2 tablespoons sugar
- 1/2 teaspoon baking soda
- 1/2 teaspoon salt
- 1 teaspoon vanilla extract (optional)

### INSTRUCTIONS:

1. In a large mixing bowl, combine the active sourdough starter, all-purpose flour, and milk. Mix well until smooth. Cover the bowl with plastic wrap or a kitchen towel and let it ferment at room temperature overnight or for at least 8 hours. This fermentation process will develop flavor and increase the leavening power of the sourdough.
2. After the fermentation period, preheat your waffle iron according to the manufacturer's instructions.
3. In a separate bowl, whisk together the melted butter (or oil), egg, sugar, baking soda, salt, and vanilla extract (if using).
4. Pour the wet ingredients into the fermented sourdough mixture and stir until well combined.
5. Lightly grease the waffle iron with cooking spray or brush it with melted butter.
6. Pour an appropriate amount of the sourdough waffle batter onto the preheated waffle iron, spreading it evenly across the surface. The amount of batter will depend on the size of your waffle iron and your preference for thickness.

7. Close the waffle iron and cook the waffles according to the manufacturer's instructions, or until they are golden brown and crispy.
8. Carefully remove the cooked waffles from the waffle iron and serve immediately, or keep them warm in a low oven until ready to serve.
9. Serve the sourdough waffles with your favorite toppings such as maple syrup, fresh berries, whipped cream, or yogurt.

Enjoy your delicious and tangy sourdough waffles!

Note: You can adjust the consistency of the batter by adding a little more milk if it's too thick or a little more flour if it's too thin. Additionally, feel free to customize the flavor by adding ingredients such as cinnamon, nutmeg, or lemon zest to the batter.

# SOURDOUGH SCONES

## CLASSIC SOURDOUGH SCONES AND ADDITIONS

**PREP TIME:** 15 minutes | **COOK TIME:** 18-20 minutes | **YIELD:** 8 scones

### INGREDIENTS:

- 1 cup all-purpose flour
- 1 cup whole wheat flour
- 1/4 cup granulated sugar
- 1/2 teaspoon salt
- 1 teaspoon baking powder
- 1/2 teaspoon baking soda
- 1/2 cup cold unsalted butter, cubed
- 1/2 cup sourdough starter, unfed (discard works perfectly here!)
- 1/2 cup buttermilk
- 1 teaspoon vanilla extract
- Zest of 1 lemon (optional)
- 1/2 cup dried fruit or chocolate chips (optional)

### CALORIES: 220 PER SERVING

Total Fat: 10g
Saturated Fat: 6g
Cholesterol: 40mg
Sodium: 230mg
Total Carbohydrate: 30g
Dietary Fiber: 1g
Sugars: 8g
Protein: 3g

### INSTRUCTIONS:

1. Preheat your oven to 400°F (200°C). Line a baking sheet with parchment paper or lightly grease it.
2. In a large mixing bowl, combine the all-purpose flour, whole wheat flour, sugar, salt, baking powder, and baking soda.
3. Add the cold butter cubes to the dry ingredients. Using a pastry cutter or your fingers, work the butter into the flour mixture until it resembles coarse crumbs with some pea-sized pieces of butter remaining.
4. In a separate bowl, mix together the sourdough starter, buttermilk, vanilla extract, and lemon zest (if using).

5. Pour the wet ingredients into the dry ingredients and stir until just combined. Be careful not to overmix.
6. If using, gently fold in the dried fruit or chocolate chips.
7. Turn the dough out onto a lightly floured surface and pat it into a circle about 1 inch thick.
8. Using a sharp knife or bench scraper, cut the circle into 8 wedges.
9. Place the scones on the prepared baking sheet, leaving some space between each one.
10. Bake for 18-20 minutes, or until the scones are golden brown on top and cooked through.
11. Allow the scones to cool on the baking sheet for a few minutes before transferring them to a wire rack to cool completely.

## VARIATIONS:

1. **Blueberry Lemon Scones**
   - Add 1 cup of fresh or frozen blueberries and 1 tablespoon of lemon zest to the dough before shaping.
2. **Cranberry Orange Scones**
   - Replace the lemon zest with orange zest and fold in 1/2 cup of dried cranberries before shaping.
3. **Chocolate Chip Scones**
   - Replace the dried fruit with 1/2 cup of chocolate chips.
4. **Savory Herb and Cheese Scones**
   - Omit the sugar and lemon zest. Add 1/2 cup of grated cheese (such as cheddar or parmesan) and 1 tablespoon of chopped fresh herbs (such as rosemary or thyme) to the dough before shaping.

These variations offer a range of flavors to suit different tastes, whether you prefer sweet or savory. Experiment with different add-ins and enjoy the delicious results of your sourdough scone creations!

# SOURDOUGH STICKY BUNS

**PREP TIME:** 20 minutes | **COOK TIME:** 25-30 minutes | **YIELD:** 8 sticky buns

### INGREDIENTS:

- 1 cup active sourdough starter
- 2 cups all-purpose flour
- 1/2 cup milk
- 1/4 cup melted butter
- 1/4 cup sugar
- 1/2 teaspoon salt
- 1/2 cup brown sugar
- 1/4 cup chopped nuts (such as pecans or walnuts)
- 2 tablespoons maple syrup

### CALORIES: 300 PER SERVING

Total Fat: 15g
Saturated Fat: 8g
Cholesterol: 45mg
Sodium: 200mg
Total Carbohydrate: 35g
Dietary Fiber: 2g
Sugars: 15g
Protein: 4g

### INSTRUCTIONS:

1. In a large mixing bowl, combine the sourdough starter, flour, milk, melted butter, sugar, and salt. Mix until a smooth dough forms.
2. Cover the bowl with a towel and let the dough rise at room temperature for 8-12 hours or overnight.
3. After the dough has risen, preheat the oven to 375°F (190°C). Grease a baking dish with butter.
4. Roll out the dough into a rectangle about 1/4 inch thick.
5. Sprinkle the brown sugar and chopped nuts evenly over the dough, then drizzle with maple syrup.
6. Roll up the dough tightly from the long side and slice it into rolls about 1 inch thick.
7. Place the rolls in the prepared baking dish, cover them with a towel, and let them rise at room temperature for 1-2 hours.
8. Bake the sticky buns for 25-30 minutes, or until golden brown and sticky.
9. Allow the buns to cool slightly before serving.

# SOURDOUGH COFFEE CAKE

**PREP TIME:** 15 minutes | **COOK TIME:** 25-30 minutes | **YIELD:** 9x9-inch coffee cake

### INGREDIENTS:

- 1 cup active sourdough starter
- 2 cups all-purpose flour
- 1/2 cup sugar
- 1/2 cup milk
- 1/4 cup melted butter
- 1 egg
- 1 teaspoon vanilla extract
- 1 teaspoon baking powder
- 1/2 teaspoon baking soda
- 1/4 teaspoon salt

### For the topping:

- 1/4 cup all-purpose flour
- 1/4 cup brown sugar
- 2 tablespoons melted butter
- 1 teaspoon ground cinnamon

### CALORIES: 280 PER SERVING

Total Fat: 12g
Saturated Fat: 7g
Cholesterol: 55mg
Sodium: 220mg
Total Carbohydrate: 35g
Dietary Fiber: 1g
Sugars: 20g
Protein: 4g

### INSTRUCTIONS:

1. Preheat the oven to 350°F (175°C) and grease a 9x9-inch baking dish.
2. In a large mixing bowl, combine the sourdough starter, flour, sugar, milk, melted butter, egg, and vanilla extract. Mix until well combined.
3. Add the baking powder, baking soda, and salt to the bowl, and mix until just combined.
4. In a separate bowl, prepare the topping by combining the flour, brown sugar, melted butter, and ground cinnamon until crumbly.
5. Pour the batter into the prepared baking dish and spread it out evenly.
6. Sprinkle the topping evenly over the batter.
7. Bake the coffee cake for 25-30 minutes, or until a toothpick inserted into the center comes out clean.
8. 8. Allow the coffee cake to cool slightly before serving.

# SOURDOUGH DANISH PASTRIES

**PREP TIME:** 20 minutes | **COOK TIME:** 15-20 minutes | **YIELD:** Approximately 12 Danish pastries

### INGREDIENTS:

- 1 cup active sourdough starter
- 2 cups all-purpose flour
- 1/2 cup milk
- 1/4 cup melted butter
- 1/4 cup sugar
- 1 egg
- 1 teaspoon vanilla extract
- 1/2 teaspoon salt

### For the filling:

- 1/4 cup cream cheese, softened
- 1/4 cup fruit preserves (such as raspberry or apricot)
- 1/4 cup chopped nuts or chocolate chips (optional)

### For the glaze:

- 1 cup powdered sugar
- 2 tablespoons milk
- 1/2 teaspoon vanilla extract

### CALORIES: 290 PER SERVING

Total Fat: 15g
Saturated Fat: 8g
Cholesterol: 60mg
Sodium: 220mg
Total Carbohydrate: 35g
Dietary Fiber: 1g
Sugars: 15g
Protein: 4g

### INSTRUCTIONS:

1. In a large mixing bowl, combine the sourdough starter, flour, milk, melted butter, sugar, egg, and vanilla extract. Mix until a smooth dough forms.
2. Cover the bowl with a towel and let the dough rise at room temperature for 8-12 hours or overnight.
3. After the dough has risen, preheat the oven to 375°F (190°C). Line a baking sheet with parchment paper.
4. Roll out the dough on a floured surface into a rectangle about 1/4 inch thick.
5. Cut the dough into squares, then cut each square diagonally to form triangles.

6. Spread a small spoonful of cream cheese and fruit preserves onto each triangle of dough, then sprinkle with chopped nuts or chocolate chips, if using.
7. Roll up each triangle starting from the wide end to form a crescent shape.
8. Place the pastries on the prepared baking sheet and let them rise at room temperature for 1-2 hours.
9. Bake the pastries for 15-20 minutes, or until golden brown.
10. While the pastries are baking, prepare the glaze by whisking together the powdered sugar, milk, and vanilla extract until smooth.
11. Allow the pastries to cool slightly before drizzling them with the glaze.

# SOURDOUGH DONUTS

Let's start with the iconic classic – donuts. Imagine sinking your teeth into a perfectly fried, golden-brown ring of delight, with a hint of tanginess that sets it apart from ordinary fare. Sourdough donuts offer a unique twist on this beloved treat, adding depth of flavor and a tender texture that will keep you coming back for seconds.

**PREP TIME:** 30 minutes | **COOK TIME:** 10-15 minutes (depending on batch size)
**YIELD:** Varies (depends on size of donuts)

### INGREDIENTS:

- 1 cup active sourdough starter
- 1/2 cup whole milk, warmed
- 1/4 cup granulated sugar
- 1 large egg, beaten
- 4 tablespoons unsalted butter, melted
- 3 cups all-purpose flour
- 1/2 teaspoon salt
- Oil for frying

### CALORIES: APPROXIMATELY 250

Total Fat: Approximately 10g
Saturated Fat: Approximately 5g
Cholesterol: Approximately 35mg
Sodium: Approximately 120mg
Total Carbohydrate: Approximately 35g
Dietary Fiber: Approximately 1g
Sugars: Approximately 5g
Protein: Approximately 5g

### INSTRUCTIONS:

1. In a large mixing bowl, combine the active sourdough starter, warm milk, and granulated sugar. Mix well.
2. Add the beaten egg and melted butter to the mixture, stirring until combined.
3. Gradually add the flour and salt, mixing until a soft dough forms.
4. Cover the dough with a clean kitchen towel and let it rest for 1-2 hours, or until it doubles in size.
5. On a floured surface, roll out the dough to a 1/2-inch thickness. Use a donut cutter or a round cookie cutter to cut out donut shapes.

Sourdough Pastries

6. Place the shaped donuts on a baking sheet lined with parchment paper. Cover them with a kitchen towel and let them rise for another 30-60 minutes.
7. Heat oil in a deep fryer or large pot to 350°F (175°C). Carefully add the donuts to the hot oil, frying them for 1-2 minutes on each side, or until they are golden brown.
8. Remove the donuts from the oil and place them on a wire rack to cool.
9. Once cooled, glaze the donuts with your favorite toppings or fillings, such as classic sugar glaze, chocolate ganache, or fruit jam.

**RECIPE VARIATIONS**

But why stop at classic glazed donuts? With sourdough as our canvas, the possibilities are endless. Here are a few tantalizing variations to spark your creativity:

1. **Cinnamon Sugar Delight:** Roll your freshly fried donuts in a mixture of cinnamon and sugar for a sweet and spicy coating that will transport you to flavor heaven.
2. **Lemon Zest Infusion:** Add a burst of citrusy brightness by incorporating lemon zest into your dough. Finish with a zesty lemon glaze for a refreshing twist on a classic.
3. **Chocolate Indulgence:** Dip your donuts in rich, velvety chocolate ganache for the ultimate indulgence. For an extra flourish, sprinkle with chopped nuts or toasted coconut.
4. **Filled with Joy:** Inject your donuts with luscious fillings such as creamy custard, fruity jam, or indulgent chocolate hazelnut spread. Each bite is a delightful surprise bursting with flavor.

**SOUTHERN** SOURDOUGH

In this section, we'll dive into the rich tradition of Southern sourdough baking. From classic cornbread to savory biscuits and tangy hush puppies, these recipes capture the essence of Southern cuisine with a delightful sourdough twist. Get ready to tantalize your taste buds with these Southern-inspired sourdough creations.

List of 10 Southern Sourdough Recipes:
1. Sourdough Cornbread
2. Buttermilk Sourdough Biscuits
3. Sourdough Hush Puppies
4. Sourdough Jalapeno Cheddar Bread
5. Sourdough Biscuit Cinnamon Rolls
6. Sourdough Fried Chicken
7. Sourdough Sausage Gravy
8. Sourdough Sweet Potato Biscuits
9. Sourdough Peach Cobbler
10. Sourdough Pecan Pie

Now, let's dive into each recipe with detailed instructions and ingredient lists.

## SOURDOUGH **CORNBREAD**

**PREP TIME:** 10 minutes | **COOK TIME:** 25-30 minutes | **YIELD:** 9 servings

### INGREDIENTS:

- 1 cup cornmeal
- 1 cup all-purpose flour
- 1/4 cup granulated sugar
- 1 teaspoon baking powder
- 1/2 teaspoon baking soda
- 1 teaspoon salt
- 1 cup active sourdough starter
- 1/2 cup buttermilk
- 2 eggs
- 1/4 cup unsalted butter, melted

### CALORIES: 180 PER SERVING

Total Fat: 6g
Saturated Fat: 3.5g
Cholesterol: 45mg
Sodium: 250mg
Total Carbohydrate: 25g
Dietary Fiber: 2g
Sugars: 5g
Protein: 4g

### INSTRUCTIONS:

1. Preheat your oven to 375°F (190°C). Grease a 9x9-inch baking pan.
2. In a large mixing bowl, whisk together the cornmeal, all-purpose flour, sugar, baking powder, baking soda, and salt.
3. In a separate bowl, combine the active sourdough starter, buttermilk, eggs, and melted butter. Mix well.
4. Pour the wet ingredients into the dry ingredients and stir until just combined.
5. Pour the batter into the prepared baking pan and spread it out evenly.
6. Bake in the preheated oven for 25-30 minutes, or until golden brown and a toothpick inserted into the center comes out clean.
7. Allow the cornbread to cool slightly before slicing and serving.

# BUTTERMILK SOURDOUGH BISCUITS

**PREP TIME:** 15 minutes | **COOK TIME:** 12-15 minutes | **YIELD:** 10 biscuits

## INGREDIENTS:

- 2 cups all-purpose flour
- 1 tablespoon baking powder
- 1/2 teaspoon baking soda
- 1 teaspoon salt
- 1/2 cup unsalted butter, cold and cubed
- 1 cup active sourdough starter
- 1/2 cup buttermilk

## CALORIES: 150 PER SERVING

Total Fat: 5g
Saturated Fat: 2.5g
Cholesterol: 20mg
Sodium: 300mg
Total Carbohydrate: 20g
Dietary Fiber: 1g
Sugars: 1g
Protein: 3g

## INSTRUCTIONS:

1. Preheat your oven to 450°F (230°C). Line a baking sheet with parchment paper.
2. In a large mixing bowl, whisk together the flour, baking powder, baking soda, and salt.
3. Add the cold, cubed butter to the dry ingredients and use a pastry cutter or your fingers to work the butter into the flour mixture until it resembles coarse crumbs.
4. Add the active sourdough starter and buttermilk to the bowl. Stir until a shaggy dough forms.
5. Turn the dough out onto a lightly floured surface and gently knead it a few times until it comes together.
6. Pat the dough out to about 1-inch thickness. Use a biscuit cutter to cut out biscuits, rerolling any scraps as needed.
7. Place the biscuits onto the prepared baking sheet, leaving a little space between each one.
8. Bake in the preheated oven for 12-15 minutes, or until the biscuits are golden brown on top.
9. Remove from the oven and let cool slightly before serving.
10. Enjoy these warm, flaky biscuits with butter, jam, or gravy for a classic Southern breakfast treat!

# SOURDOUGH HUSH PUPPIES

**PREP TIME:** 15 minutes | **COOK TIME:** 2-3 minutes per batch | **YIELD:** Approx. 24 hush puppies

### INGREDIENTS:

- 1 cup cornmeal
- 1/2 cup all-purpose flour
- 1 teaspoon baking powder
- 1/2 teaspoon baking soda
- 1 teaspoon salt
- 1/2 cup active sourdough starter
- 1/2 cup buttermilk
- 1 egg
- 1/4 cup finely chopped onion
- 1/4 cup finely chopped green bell pepper
- 1/4 cup finely chopped fresh parsley
- Vegetable oil for frying

### CALORIES: 130 PER SERVING

Total Fat: 3.5g
Saturated Fat: 0.5g
Cholesterol: 15mg
Sodium: 240mg
Total Carbohydrate: 20g
Dietary Fiber: 1g
Sugars: 1g
Protein: 3g

### INSTRUCTIONS:

1. In a large mixing bowl, whisk together the cornmeal, all-purpose flour, baking powder, baking soda, and salt.
2. In a separate bowl, combine the active sourdough starter, buttermilk, and egg. Mix well.
3. Add the wet ingredients to the dry ingredients and stir until just combined.
4. Fold in the chopped onion, green bell pepper, and parsley until evenly distributed throughout the batter.
5. Heat vegetable oil in a deep fryer or heavy-bottomed pot to 350°F (175°C).
6. Drop spoonfuls of the batter into the hot oil, frying in batches to avoid overcrowding.
7. Fry the hush puppies for 2-3 minutes, or until golden brown and crispy.
8. Remove from the oil using a slotted spoon and drain on paper towels.
9. Serve the hush puppies warm with your favorite dipping sauce or alongside a Southern-inspired meal.
10. These crispy, savory bites are perfect for dipping into sauces or enjoying on their own as a delicious appetizer or side dish.

# SOURDOUGH JALAPENO CHEDDAR BREAD

**PREP TIME:** 5-8 hours | **COOK TIME:** 30-35 minutes | **YIELD:** 1 loaf

## INGREDIENTS:

- 3 cups bread flour
- 1 cup active sourdough starter
- 1 cup shredded cheddar cheese
- 1/4 cup pickled jalapeno slices, chopped
- 1 teaspoon salt
- 1/2 teaspoon garlic powder
- 1/2 teaspoon onion powder
- 1/2 teaspoon paprika
- 1 cup lukewarm water

## CALORIES: 160 PER SERVING

Total Fat: 4.5g
Saturated Fat: 2.5g
Cholesterol: 20mg
Sodium: 270mg
Total Carbohydrate: 25g
Dietary Fiber: 1g
Sugars: 2g
Protein: 5g

## INSTRUCTIONS:

1. In a large mixing bowl, combine the bread flour, active sourdough starter, shredded cheddar cheese, chopped pickled jalapenos, salt, garlic powder, onion powder, and paprika.
2. Gradually add the lukewarm water to the bowl, stirring until a shaggy dough forms.
3. Turn the dough out onto a lightly floured surface and knead for 8-10 minutes, or until the dough is smooth and elastic.
4. Place the dough back into the mixing bowl, cover with a clean kitchen towel, and let it rise at room temperature for 4-6 hours, or until doubled in size.
5. Once doubled, gently punch down the dough and shape it into a round loaf.
6. Place the shaped loaf onto a lightly floured baking sheet or into a proofing basket, cover, and let it rise for an additional 1-2 hours.
7. Preheat your oven to 450°F (230°C). If using a baking stone, place it in the oven to preheat as well.
8. Score the top of the risen loaf with a sharp knife or razor blade.
9. Transfer the loaf to the preheated oven and bake for 30-35 minutes, or until the bread is golden brown and sounds hollow when tapped on the bottom.
10. Remove from the oven and let cool on a wire rack before slicing and serving.
11. This flavorful bread pairs perfectly with soups, salads, or makes a delicious addition to any cheese board.

# SOURDOUGH BISCUIT CINNAMON ROLLS

**PREP TIME:** 1-2 hours | **COOK TIME:** 20-25 minutes | **YIELD:** 12 cinnamon rolls

## INGREDIENTS:

For the Dough:
- 2 cups all-purpose flour
- 1 tablespoon baking powder
- 1/2 teaspoon baking soda
- 1 teaspoon salt
- 1/2 cup unsalted butter, cold and cubed
- 1 cup active sourdough starter
- 1/2 cup buttermilk

For the Filling:
- 1/2 cup brown sugar
- 2 teaspoons ground cinnamon
- 1/4 cup unsalted butter, softened

For the Glaze:
- 1 cup powdered sugar
- 2-3 tablespoons milk
- 1 teaspoon vanilla extract

**CALORIES: 200 PER SERVING**

Total Fat: 7g
Saturated Fat: 3.5g
Cholesterol: 25mg
Sodium: 220mg
Total Carbohydrate: 30g
Dietary Fiber: 1g
Sugars: 10g
Protein: 4g

## INSTRUCTIONS:

1. In a large mixing bowl, whisk together the flour, baking powder, baking soda, and salt.
2. Add the cold, cubed butter to the dry ingredients and use a pastry cutter or your fingers to work the butter into the flour mixture until it resembles coarse crumbs.
3. Add the active sourdough starter and buttermilk to the bowl. Stir until a shaggy dough forms.
4. Turn the dough out onto a lightly floured surface and gently knead it a few times until it comes together.
5. Roll the dough out into a rectangle, about 1/4 inch thick.

6. Spread the softened butter evenly over the surface of the dough.
7. In a small bowl, mix together the brown sugar and ground cinnamon for the filling. Sprinkle the mixture evenly over the buttered dough.
8. Starting from one long edge, tightly roll the dough into a log.
9. Use a sharp knife to slice the log into 12 equal pieces.
10. Place the sliced rolls into a greased baking dish, leaving a little space between each one.
11. Cover the dish with plastic wrap and let the rolls rise at room temperature for 1-2 hours, or until doubled in size.
12. Preheat your oven to 375°F (190°C).
13. Bake the risen rolls in the preheated oven for 20-25 minutes, or until golden brown and cooked through.
14. While the rolls are baking, prepare the glaze by whisking together the powdered sugar, milk, and vanilla extract until smooth.
15. Remove the rolls from the oven and let cool for a few minutes before drizzling with the glaze.
16. These soft and gooey cinnamon rolls are perfect for a special breakfast or brunch treat.

# SOURDOUGH FRIED CHICKEN

**PREP TIME:** 10 minutes, plus marinating time
**COOK TIME:** 15-20 minutes | **YIELD:** 4 servings

### INGREDIENTS:

- 4 bone-in, skin-on chicken thighs
- 1 cup active sourdough starter
- 1 cup buttermilk
- 1 teaspoon salt
- 1 teaspoon paprika
- 1/2 teaspoon garlic powder
- 1/2 teaspoon onion powder
- Vegetable oil for frying

### CALORIES: 280 PER SERVING

Total Fat: 15g
Saturated Fat: 3.5g
Cholesterol: 75mg
Sodium: 320mg
Total Carbohydrate: 15g
Dietary Fiber: 0g
Sugars: 0g
Protein: 22g

### INSTRUCTIONS:

1. In a large bowl, whisk together the active sourdough starter, buttermilk, salt, paprika, garlic powder, and onion powder.
2. Add the chicken thighs to the bowl, making sure they are fully submerged in the marinade. Cover and refrigerate for at least 4 hours, or overnight.
3. Remove the chicken from the refrigerator and let it come to room temperature for about 30 minutes before frying.
4. Heat vegetable oil in a large skillet or Dutch oven to 350°F (175°C).
5. Remove the chicken from the marinade, allowing any excess to drip off.
6. Carefully place the chicken thighs into the hot oil, skin-side down, being careful not to overcrowd the pan.
7. Fry the chicken thighs for 6-8 minutes per side, or until golden brown and cooked through. The internal temperature should reach 165°F (74°C).
8. Remove the fried chicken from the oil and transfer to a wire rack or paper towels to drain any excess oil.
9. Let the chicken rest for a few minutes before serving.
10. This Southern-inspired sourdough fried chicken is crispy on the outside, juicy on the inside, and packed with flavor.

# SOURDOUGH SAUSAGE GRAVY

**PREP TIME:** 5 minutes  |  **COOK TIME:** 15 minutes  |  **YIELD:** 4 servings

### INGREDIENTS:

- 1/2 pound breakfast sausage
- 2 tablespoons unsalted butter
- 1/4 cup all-purpose flour
- 2 cups whole milk
- 1 cup active sourdough starter
- Salt and pepper to taste

### CALORIES: 160 PER SERVING

Total Fat: 10g
Saturated Fat: 5g
Cholesterol: 30mg
Sodium: 330mg
Total Carbohydrate: 10g
Dietary Fiber: 0g
Sugars: 1g
Protein: 7g

### INSTRUCTIONS:

1. In a large skillet, cook the breakfast sausage over medium heat until browned and cooked through, breaking it up into crumbles with a spoon as it cooks.
2. Once the sausage is cooked, add the unsalted butter to the skillet and melt it with the sausage.
3. Sprinkle the flour over the sausage and butter mixture. Stir to combine and cook for 1-2 minutes to cook out the raw flour taste.
4. Gradually pour in the whole milk, stirring constantly to prevent lumps from forming.
5. Add the active sourdough starter to the skillet and stir until well combined.
6. Continue cooking the gravy over medium heat, stirring frequently, until it thickens to your desired consistency. This should take about 5-7 minutes.
7. Season the gravy with salt and pepper to taste.
8. Serve the sourdough sausage gravy hot over biscuits, toast, or fried chicken for a hearty Southern breakfast or brunch

## SOURDOUGH SWEET POTATO BISCUITS

**PREP TIME:** Approximately 15 minutes
**COOK TIME:** 12-15 minutes | **YIELD:** Makes about 12 biscuits

### INGREDIENTS:

- 1 cup mashed sweet potato
- 1/2 cup active sourdough starter
- 2 cups all-purpose flour
- 1/4 cup unsalted butter, melted
- 1/4 cup buttermilk
- 2 tablespoons honey
- 1 teaspoon baking powder
- 1/2 teaspoon baking soda
- 1/2 teaspoon salt

**CALORIES: 170 PER SERVING**

Total Fat: 7g
Saturated Fat: 4g
Cholesterol: 20mg
Sodium: 220mg
Total Carbohydrate: 25g
Dietary Fiber: 2g
Sugars: 3g
Protein: 3g

### INSTRUCTIONS:

1. Preheat your oven to 425°F (220°C) and grease a baking sheet.
2. In a large mixing bowl, combine the mashed sweet potato, active sourdough starter, melted butter, buttermilk, and honey. Mix until well combined.
3. In a separate bowl, sift together the flour, baking powder, baking soda, and salt.
4. Gradually add the dry ingredients to the wet ingredients, mixing until a soft dough forms.
5. Turn the dough out onto a floured surface and knead gently for a minute or two.
6. Roll out the dough to about 1/2 inch thickness and cut out biscuits using a round cutter.
7. Place the biscuits on the prepared baking sheet and bake for 12-15 minutes, or until golden brown.
8. Remove from the oven and let cool slightly before serving.
9. These tender and flavorful sourdough sweet potato biscuits are the perfect addition to any Southern meal, whether enjoyed with butter and honey for breakfast or alongside savory dishes for dinner.

## SOURDOUGH PEACH COBBLER

**PREP TIME:** Approximately 20 minutes
**COOK TIME:** 40-45 minutes  |  **YIELD:** Makes about 8 servings

### INGREDIENTS:

- 4 cups sliced fresh peaches
- 1 cup granulated sugar
- 1 tablespoon lemon juice
- 1/2 teaspoon ground cinnamon
- 1/4 teaspoon ground nutmeg
- 1/4 cup all-purpose flour
- 1/2 cup unsalted butter
- 1 cup all-purpose flour
- 1/2 cup granulated sugar
- 1/2 cup sourdough starter
- 1/2 cup milk
- 1 teaspoon vanilla extract
- 1/2 teaspoon baking powder
- 1/4 teaspoon salt

### CALORIES: 210 PER SERVING

Total Fat: 8g
Saturated Fat: 4g
Cholesterol: 20mg
Sodium: 180mg
Total Carbohydrate: 35g
Dietary Fiber: 2g
Sugars: 20g
Protein: 2g

### INSTRUCTIONS:

1. Preheat your oven to 350°F (175°C).
2. In a mixing bowl, combine the sliced peaches, granulated sugar, lemon juice, ground cinnamon, ground nutmeg, and 1/4 cup flour. Toss until the peaches are evenly coated.
3. Transfer the peach mixture to a greased baking dish.
4. In a saucepan, melt the unsalted butter over medium heat.

5. In a separate mixing bowl, combine the remaining flour, granulated sugar, sourdough starter, milk, vanilla extract, baking powder, and salt. Mix until smooth.
6. Pour the sourdough batter over the peaches in the baking dish.
7. Drizzle the melted butter over the top of the batter.
8. Bake in the preheated oven for 40-45 minutes, or until the cobbler is golden brown and bubbly.
9. Remove from the oven and let cool slightly before serving.

This irresistible sourdough peach cobbler is best enjoyed warm, topped with a scoop of vanilla ice cream for the ultimate Southern dessert experience.

# SOURDOUGH PECAN PIE

**PREP TIME:** Approximately 15 minutes
**COOK TIME:** 50-60 minutes | **YIELD:** Makes 1 pie, approximately 8 servings

## INGREDIENTS:

- 1 prepared pie crust (homemade or store-bought)
- 1 cup granulated sugar
- 1 cup light corn syrup
- 3 eggs
- 1/4 cup unsalted butter, melted
- 1 teaspoon vanilla extract
- 1 cup chopped pecans
- 1/2 cup sourdough starter
- 1 tablespoon all-purpose flour
- 1/4 teaspoon salt

## CALORIES: 300 PER SERVING

Total Fat: 18g
Saturated Fat: 5g
Cholesterol: 50mg
Sodium: 200mg
Total Carbohydrate: 35g
Dietary Fiber: 2g
Sugars: 25g
Protein: 4g

## INSTRUCTIONS:

1. Preheat your oven to 350°F (175°C).
2. Place the prepared pie crust in a 9-inch pie dish and crimp the edges.
3. In a mixing bowl, whisk together the granulated sugar, light corn syrup, eggs, melted butter, and vanilla extract until smooth.
4. Stir in the chopped pecans, sourdough starter, flour, and salt until well combined.
5. Pour the pecan mixture into the prepared pie crust.
6. Place the pie in the preheated oven and bake for 50-60 minutes, or until the filling is set and the crust is golden brown.
7. Remove from the oven and let cool completely before slicing and serving.
8. This classic sourdough pecan pie is a Southern favorite, with its rich, gooey filling and crunchy pecans, making it the perfect dessert for any occasion. Serve it with a dollop of whipped cream or a scoop of vanilla ice cream for a truly indulgent treat.

# SOURDOUGH PIE CRUST

**PREP TIME:** 15 minutes (plus at least 1 hour chilling time)
**COOK TIME:** Depends on the pie recipe | **YIELD:** Makes 2 pie crusts

## INGREDIENTS:

1 cup active sourdough starter
2 1/2 cups all-purpose flour
1 teaspoon salt
1/2 cup cold unsalted butter, cubed
4-6 tablespoons ice water

## CALORIES: APPROXIMATELY 160 PER SERVING (1/8 OF CRUST)

Total Fat: Approximately 8g
Saturated Fat: Approximately 5g
Cholesterol: Approximately 20mg
Sodium: Approximately 200mg
Total Carbohydrate: Approximately 19g
Dietary Fiber: Approximately 1g
Sugars: Approximately 0g
Protein: Approximately 2g

## INSTRUCTIONS:

1. In a large mixing bowl, combine the active sourdough starter, all-purpose flour, and salt.
2. Add the cold cubed butter to the flour mixture. Using a pastry cutter or your fingers, work the butter into the flour until the mixture resembles coarse crumbs.
3. Gradually add ice water, 1 tablespoon at a time, mixing with a fork until the dough begins to come together.
4. Turn the dough out onto a lightly floured surface and knead gently until it forms a cohesive ball. Be careful not to overwork the dough.
5. Divide the dough into two equal portions and shape each portion into a disk. Wrap each disk tightly in plastic wrap and refrigerate for at least 1 hour, or until firm.
6. When ready to use, remove the dough from the refrigerator and let it sit at room temperature for about 10-15 minutes to slightly soften.
7. Roll out the dough on a lightly floured surface to fit your pie dish. Carefully transfer the rolled-out dough to the pie dish and press it gently into the bottom and sides.
8. Trim any excess dough hanging over the edges of the pie dish and crimp the edges as desired.
9. Fill the pie crust with your desired filling and bake according to your pie recipe instructions.

# ITALIAN INSPIRED
## SOURDOUGH RECIPES

Now we embark on a culinary journey through Italy with a twist – sourdough! From rustic focaccia to decadent tiramisu, these recipes infuse the flavors of Italy with the tangy goodness of sourdough. Get ready to bring a taste of Italy into your kitchen with these ten delightful recipes.

List of 10 Italian Sourdough Recipes:

1. [Sourdough Focaccia with Rosemary and Sea Salt]
2. [Rustic Sourdough Pizza with Fresh Mozzarella and Basil]
3. [Sourdough Ciabatta Bread with Sundried Tomatoes and Herbs]
4. [Sourdough Olive Bread with Kalamata Olives and Thyme]
5. [Sourdough Caprese Bread with Cherry Tomatoes, Mozzarella, and Basil]
6. [Sourdough Parmesan Garlic Breadsticks]
7. [Sourdough Panettone with Dried Fruit and Nuts]
8. [Sourdough Risotto-Stuffed Tomatoes]
9. [Sourdough Tiramisu with Espresso and Mascarpone]
10. [Sourdough Cannoli with Sweet Ricotta Filling and Chocolate Chips]

# SOURDOUGH FOCACCIA WITH ROSEMARY

**PREP TIME:** 15 minutes (plus 4-6 hours rising time)
**COOK TIME:** 20-25 minutes | **YIELD:** Makes 1 large focaccia

### INGREDIENTS:

- 1 cup active sourdough starter
- 2 1/2 cups bread flour
- 1 cup warm water
- 2 tablespoons olive oil
- 1 tablespoon honey
- 1 teaspoon salt
- Fresh rosemary sprigs
- Coarse sea salt

### CALORIES: 200 PER SERVING

Total Fat: 7g
Saturated Fat: 1g
Cholesterol: 0mg
Sodium: 400mg
Total Carbohydrate: 30g
Dietary Fiber: 2g
Sugars: 0g
Protein: 5g

### INSTRUCTIONS:

1. In a large mixing bowl, combine the sourdough starter, bread flour, warm water, olive oil, honey, and salt. Knead until a smooth dough forms.
2. Cover the bowl and let the dough rise at room temperature for 4-6 hours, until doubled in size.
3. Preheat the oven to 450°F (230°C). Punch down the dough and transfer it to a greased baking sheet.
4. Press the dough into a rectangle or circle shape, about 1 inch thick.
5. Use your fingers to make dimples on the dough's surface. Drizzle with olive oil and sprinkle with fresh rosemary leaves and coarse sea salt.
6. Bake for 20-25 minutes, or until golden brown and crispy on the outside.
7. Serve warm, drizzled with additional olive oil if desired.

# RUSTIC SOURDOUGH **PIZZA** WITH **FRESH MOZZARELLA** AND **BASIL**

**PREP TIME:** 15 minutes (plus 4-6 hours rising time)
**COOK TIME:** 12-15 minutes  |  **YIELD:** Makes 2 pizzas

## INGREDIENTS:

- 1 cup active sourdough starter
- 2 cups bread flour
- 1/2 cup warm water
- 2 tablespoons olive oil
- 1 teaspoon salt
- Pizza sauce
- Fresh mozzarella cheese, sliced
- Fresh basil leaves

Optional toppings:

- sliced tomatoes, olives, peppers, mushrooms

### CALORIES: 280 PER SERVING

Total Fat: 12g
Saturated Fat: 6g
Cholesterol: 30mg
Sodium: 500mg
Total Carbohydrate: 30g
Dietary Fiber: 2g
Sugars: 2g
Protein: 12g

## INSTRUCTIONS:

1. In a large mixing bowl, combine the sourdough starter, bread flour, warm water, olive oil, and salt. Knead until a smooth dough forms.
2. Cover the bowl and let the dough rise at room temperature for 4-6 hours, until doubled in size.
3. Preheat the oven to 500°F (260°C). Punch down the dough and divide it into two equal portions.
4. Roll out each portion of dough on a floured surface to your desired thickness.
5. Transfer the dough to a greased baking sheet or pizza stone. Spread pizza sauce over the dough and top with fresh mozzarella slices and any desired toppings.
6. Bake for 12-15 minutes, or until the crust is golden brown and the cheese is bubbly.
7. Remove from the oven and sprinkle with fresh basil leaves before serving.

# SOURDOUGH CIABATTA BREAD WITH SUNDRIED TOMATOES AND HERBS

**PREP TIME:** 15 minutes (plus 8-12 hours rising time)
**COOK TIME:** 20-25 minutes | **YIELD:** Makes 1 loaf

### INGREDIENTS:

- 1 cup active sourdough starter
- 2 1/2 cups bread flour
- 1 cup warm water
- 2 tablespoons olive oil
- 1 teaspoon salt
- 1/2 cup sundried tomatoes, chopped
- 2 tablespoons fresh herbs (such as basil, oregano, or thyme), chopped

### CALORIES: 180 PER SERVING

Total Fat: 1.5g
Saturated Fat: 0.5g
Cholesterol: 0mg
Sodium: 350mg
Total Carbohydrate: 35g
Dietary Fiber: 2g
Sugars: 1g
Protein: 5g

### INSTRUCTIONS:

1. In a large mixing bowl, combine the sourdough starter, bread flour, warm water, olive oil, and salt. Knead until a sticky dough forms.
2. Cover the bowl and let the dough rise at room temperature for 8-12 hours, until doubled in size and bubbly.
3. Preheat the oven to 450°F (230°C). Punch down the dough and transfer it to a greased baking sheet.
4. Shape the dough into a rough rectangle or oval shape, about 1 inch thick.
5. Press the chopped sundried tomatoes and fresh herbs into the surface of the dough.
6. Bake for 25-30 minutes, or until the crust is golden brown and crispy.
7. Allow the ciabatta bread to cool slightly before slicing and serving.

# SOURDOUGH **OLIVE BREAD** WITH **KALAMATA OLIVES** AND **THYME**

**PREP TIME:** 15 minutes (plus 8-12 hours rising time)
**COOK TIME:** 30-35 minutes | **YIELD:** Makes 1 loaf

### INGREDIENTS:

- 1 cup active sourdough starter
- 2 1/2 cups bread flour
- 1 cup warm water
- 2 tablespoons olive oil
- 1 teaspoon salt
- 1/2 cup Kalamata olives, pitted and chopped
- 1 tablespoon fresh thyme leaves

### CALORIES: 160 PER SERVING

Total Fat: 6g
Saturated Fat: 1g
Cholesterol: 0mg
Sodium: 300mg
Total Carbohydrate: 25g
Dietary Fiber: 2g
Sugars: 1g
Protein: 4g

### INSTRUCTIONS:

1. In a large mixing bowl, combine the sourdough starter, bread flour, warm water, olive oil, and salt. Knead until a smooth dough forms.
2. Cover the bowl and let the dough rise at room temperature for 8-12 hours, until doubled in size and bubbly.
3. Preheat the oven to 450°F (230°C). Punch down the dough and transfer it to a greased baking sheet.
4. Shape the dough into a round loaf and place it on the baking sheet.
5. Press the chopped Kalamata olives and fresh thyme leaves into the surface of the dough.
6. Bake for 30-35 minutes, or until the crust is golden brown and sounds hollow when tapped on the bottom.
7. Allow the olive bread to cool completely before slicing and serving.

## SOURDOUGH **CAPRESE BREAD** WITH **CHERRY TOMATOES, MOZZARELLA,** AND **BASIL**

**PREP TIME:** 15 minutes (plus 8-12 hours rising time)
**COOK TIME:** 30-35 minutes | **YIELD:** Makes 1 loaf

### INGREDIENTS:

- 1 cup active sourdough starter
- 2 1/2 cups bread flour
- 1 cup warm water
- 2 tablespoons olive oil
- 1 teaspoon salt
- 1 cup cherry tomatoes, halved
- 1 cup fresh mozzarella cheese, diced
- 1/4 cup fresh basil leaves, chopped

### CALORIES: 190 PER SERVING

Total Fat: 7g
Saturated Fat: 3.5g
Cholesterol: 20mg
Sodium: 350mg
Total Carbohydrate: 25g
Dietary Fiber: 2g
Sugars: 2g
Protein: 8g

### INSTRUCTIONS:

1. In a large mixing bowl, combine the sourdough starter, bread flour, warm water, olive oil, and salt. Knead until a smooth dough forms.
2. Cover the bowl and let the dough rise at room temperature for 8-12 hours, until doubled in size and bubbly.
3. Preheat the oven to 450°F (230°C). Punch down the dough and transfer it to a greased baking sheet.
4. Shape the dough into a round loaf and place it on the baking sheet.
5. Press the cherry tomato halves, diced mozzarella cheese, and chopped basil leaves into the surface of the dough.
6. Bake for 30-35 minutes, or until the crust is golden brown and sounds hollow when tapped on the bottom.
7. Allow the Caprese bread to cool slightly before slicing and serving.

# SOURDOUGH PARMESAN GARLIC BREADSTICKS

**PREP TIME:** 120 minutes (plus 1-2 hours rising time)
**COOK TIME:** 15-20 minutes | **YIELD:** Makes approximately 12 breadsticks

### INGREDIENTS:

- 1 cup active sourdough starter
- 2 cups all-purpose flour
- 1/2 cup grated Parmesan cheese
- 1/4 cup melted butter
- 2 cloves garlic, minced
- 1 teaspoon dried oregano
- 1/2 teaspoon salt
- 1/4 teaspoon black pepper
- Additional grated Parmesan cheese for topping

### CALORIES: 150 PER SERVING

Total Fat: 5g
Saturated Fat: 2.5g
Cholesterol: 10mg
Sodium: 280mg
Total Carbohydrate: 20g
Dietary Fiber: 1g
Sugars: 1g
Protein: 4g

### INSTRUCTIONS:

1. In a large mixing bowl, combine the sourdough starter, flour, grated Parmesan cheese, melted butter, minced garlic, dried oregano, salt, and black pepper. Mix until a smooth dough forms.
2. Divide the dough into equal portions and roll each portion into a thin rope shape.
3. Place the ropes onto a baking sheet lined with parchment paper, leaving space between each one.
4. Cover the breadsticks with a towel and let them rise at room temperature for 1-2 hours.
5. Preheat the oven to 375°F (190°C). Brush the breadsticks with melted butter and sprinkle additional grated Parmesan cheese on top.
6. Bake the breadsticks for 15-20 minutes, or until golden brown and crispy.
7. Serve the breadsticks warm with marinara sauce for dipping.

# SOURDOUGH PANETTONE WITH DRIED FRUIT AND NUTS

**PREP TIME:** 20 minutes (plus 6-8 hours rising time)
**COOK TIME:** 40-50 minutes | **YIELD:** Makes 1 panettone

### INGREDIENTS:

- 1 cup active sourdough starter
- 3 cups all-purpose flour
- 1/2 cup sugar
- 1/2 cup melted butter
- 3 eggs
- 1/2 cup milk
- 1 teaspoon vanilla extract
- 1/2 teaspoon salt
- 1/2 cup mixed dried fruit (such as raisins, currants, and chopped apricots)
- 1/2 cup chopped nuts (such as almonds or walnuts)
- Zest of 1 lemon
- Zest of 1 orange

### CALORIES: 280 PER SERVING

Total Fat: 8g
Saturated Fat: 4g
Cholesterol: 45mg
Sodium: 220mg
Total Carbohydrate: 45g
Dietary Fiber: 2g
Sugars: 25g
Protein: 6g

### INSTRUCTIONS:

1. In a large mixing bowl, combine the sourdough starter, flour, sugar, melted butter, eggs, milk, vanilla extract, and salt. Mix until well combined.
2. Fold in the mixed dried fruit, chopped nuts, lemon zest, and orange zest until evenly distributed throughout the dough.
3. Transfer the dough to a greased panettone mold or a large, tall baking dish lined with parchment paper.
4. Cover the dough with a towel and let it rise at room temperature for 6-8 hours or until doubled in size.
5. Preheat the oven to 350°F (175°C). Bake the panettone for 40-50 minutes, or until golden brown and a toothpick inserted into the center comes out clean.
6. Allow the panettone to cool completely before slicing and serving.

# SOURDOUGH RISOTTO-STUFFED TOMATOES

**PREP TIME:** 20 minutes | **COOK TIME:** 50 minutes | **YIELD:** 4 servings

## INGREDIENTS:

- 4 large tomatoes
- 1 cup Arborio rice
- 2 cups chicken or vegetable broth
- 1/2 cup dry white wine
- 1/2 cup grated Parmesan cheese
- 2 tablespoons olive oil
- 2 cloves garlic, minced
- 1/2 cup diced onion
- 1/2 cup diced bell pepper
- 1/2 cup diced zucchini
- 1/2 cup diced mushrooms
- 1/4 cup chopped fresh basil
- Salt and pepper to taste

### CALORIES: 150 PER SERVING

Total Fat: 5g
Saturated Fat: 1.5g
Cholesterol: 10mg
Sodium: 250mg
Total Carbohydrate: 25g
Dietary Fiber: 3g
Sugars: 4g
Protein: 5g

## INSTRUCTIONS:

1. Preheat the oven to 375°F (190°C). Slice off the tops of the tomatoes and scoop out the seeds and pulp to create hollow shells. Set aside.
2. In a large skillet, heat the olive oil over medium heat. Add the minced garlic and diced onion, and cook until softened.
3. Stir in the Arborio rice and cook for 1-2 minutes, until lightly toasted.
4. Pour in the white wine and cook until it has been absorbed by the rice.
5. Gradually add the chicken or vegetable broth, 1/2 cup at a time, stirring constantly and allowing each addition to be absorbed before adding more.

6. When the rice is almost tender, stir in the diced bell pepper, zucchini, mushrooms, and chopped fresh basil. Cook for an additional 2-3 minutes.
7. Remove the skillet from the heat and stir in the grated Parmesan cheese. Season with salt and pepper to taste.
8. Stuff the risotto mixture into the hollowed-out tomatoes and place them in a baking dish.
9. Bake the stuffed tomatoes for 25-30 minutes, or until the tomatoes are tender and the filling is heated through.

# SOURDOUGH TIRAMISU WITH ESPRESSO AND MASCARPONE

**PREP TIME:** 30 minutes | **COOK TIME:** 25 minutes (for baking the sourdough cake)
**CHILL TIME:** At least 4 hours | **YIELD:** 8 servings

### INGREDIENTS:

- 1 cup active sourdough starter
- 2 cups all-purpose flour
- 1/2 cup sugar
- 1/2 cup milk
- 1/4 cup melted butter
- 2 eggs
- 1 teaspoon vanilla extract
- 1/2 teaspoon baking powder
- 1/4 teaspoon salt
- 1 cup strong brewed coffee or espresso, cooled
- 1/4 cup coffee liqueur (optional)
- 8 ounces mascarpone cheese
- 1/2 cup powdered sugar
- Cocoa powder for dusting
- Ladyfinger cookies (store-bought or homemade)

### CALORIES: 300 PER SERVING

Total Fat: 15g
Saturated Fat: 9g
Cholesterol: 100mg
Sodium: 50mg
Total Carbohydrate: 35g
Dietary Fiber: 0g
Sugars: 20g
Protein: 4g

### INSTRUCTIONS:

1. Preheat the oven to 350°F (175°C). Grease a 9x13-inch baking dish.
2. In a large mixing bowl, combine the sourdough starter, flour, sugar, milk, melted butter, eggs, vanilla extract, baking powder, and salt. Mix until a smooth batter forms.
3. Pour the batter into the prepared baking dish and spread it out evenly.

Italian Inspired | 85

4. Bake the sourdough cake for 20-25 minutes, or until golden brown and a toothpick inserted into the center comes out clean. Allow the cake to cool completely.
5. In a shallow dish, combine the cooled brewed coffee or espresso with the coffee liqueur, if using.
6. In a separate mixing bowl, whisk together the mascarpone cheese and powdered sugar until smooth and creamy.
7. Cut the cooled sourdough cake into squares or rectangles that will fit into your serving dish.
8. Dip each piece of sourdough cake briefly into the coffee mixture, making sure not to soak it too long to avoid it becoming soggy.
9. Arrange a layer of soaked sourdough cake in the bottom of your serving dish.
10. Spread a layer of the mascarpone mixture over the soaked sourdough cake.
11. Repeat the layers of soaked sourdough cake and mascarpone mixture until all the ingredients are used, finishing with a layer of mascarpone on top.
12. Cover the tiramisu with plastic wrap and refrigerate for at least 4 hours, or overnight, to allow the flavors to meld.
13. Before serving, dust the top of the tiramisu with cocoa powder. Enjoy chilled!

# SOURDOUGH **CANNOLI** WITH **SWEET RICOTTA FILLING** AND **CHOCOLATE CHIPS**

**PREP TIME:** 1 hour 30 minutes (including chilling time)
**COOK TIME:** 20 minutes | **YIELD:** Makes about 12 cannoli

### INGREDIENTS:

- 1 cup active sourdough starter
- 2 cups all-purpose flour
- 1/4 cup sugar
- 1/4 cup melted butter
- 1/4 cup Marsala wine (or substitute with milk)
- 1 teaspoon cocoa powder
- 1/2 teaspoon cinnamon
- Pinch of salt
- Vegetable oil, for frying
- 1 cup ricotta cheese
- 1/4 cup powdered sugar
- 1/2 teaspoon vanilla extract
- 1/4 cup mini chocolate chips
- Powdered sugar, for dusting

**CALORIES: 220 PER SERVING**

Total Fat: 10g
Saturated Fat: 6g
Cholesterol: 20mg
Sodium: 90mg
Total Carbohydrate: 30g
Dietary Fiber: 1g
Sugars: 15g
Protein: 4g

### INSTRUCTIONS:

1. In a large mixing bowl, combine the sourdough starter, flour, sugar, melted butter, Marsala wine, cocoa powder, cinnamon, and salt. Mix until a smooth dough forms. If the dough is too dry, add a little more wine or milk as needed.
2. Wrap the dough in plastic wrap and let it rest in the refrigerator for at least 1 hour, or overnight.
3. After the dough has chilled, divide it into smaller portions and roll each portion out into a thin circle on a lightly floured surface. The circles should be about 5-6 inches in diameter.

Italian Inspired

4. Wrap each circle of dough around a cannoli form or a metal cannoli tube, overlapping the edges slightly and sealing them with a little water.
5. Heat vegetable oil in a deep fryer or heavy-bottomed pot to 350°F (175°C).
6. Carefully place the wrapped cannoli tubes into the hot oil, a few at a time, and fry until golden brown and crispy, about 3-4 minutes.
7. Remove the fried cannoli shells from the oil using tongs or a slotted spoon and transfer them to a wire rack set over a paper towel-lined baking sheet to drain and cool completely.
8. In a mixing bowl, combine the ricotta cheese, powdered sugar, and vanilla extract. Mix until smooth and creamy.
9. Fold in the mini chocolate chips until evenly distributed throughout the filling.
10. Once the cannoli shells have cooled, carefully slide them off the metal tubes. Fill each shell with the sweet ricotta filling using a piping bag or spoon.
11. Dust the filled cannoli with powdered sugar just before serving.
12. Enjoy these homemade sourdough cannoli as a delicious and indulgent treat!
13. With these fun and flavorful sourdough Italian recipes, you'll bring a taste of Italy into your kitchen and delight your family and friends with each bite!

**MEDITERRANEAN** INSPIRED
SOURDOUGH RECIPES

Now it's time we explore the vibrant and flavorful world of Mediterranean-inspired sourdough recipes. From savory flatbreads to aromatic dips, these dishes will transport your taste buds to the sunny shores of the Mediterranean. Get ready to infuse your sourdough baking with a touch of Mediterranean flair!

List of 10 Italian Sourdough Recipes:
1. Sourdough Focaccia with Herbs
2. Sourdough Greek Flatbread (Pita)
3. Sourdough Olive Bread
4. Sourdough Mediterranean Pizza
5. Sourdough Spanakopita
6. Sourdough Stuffed Grape Leaves (Dolmades)
7. Sourdough Mediterranean Flatbread (Lahmacun)
8. Sourdough Greek Salad
9. Sourdough Hummus
10. Sourdough Tabbouleh Salad

## SOURDOUGH **FOCACCIA** WITH **HERBS**

**PREP TIME:** Approximately 4-6 hours (including rising time)
**COOK TIME:** 20-25 minutes | **YIELD:** 1 focaccia, about 8 servings

### INGREDIENTS:

- 1 cup active sourdough starter
- 2 cups bread flour
- 1 cup warm water
- 2 tablespoons olive oil
- 1 teaspoon salt
- 2 cloves garlic, minced
- 2 tablespoons fresh rosemary, chopped
- Coarse sea salt, for topping

### CALORIES: 200 PER SERVING

Total Fat: 7g
Saturated Fat: 1g
Cholesterol: 0mg
Sodium: 400mg
Total Carbohydrate: 30g
Dietary Fiber: 2g
Sugars: 0g
Protein: 5g

### INSTRUCTIONS:

1. In a large mixing bowl, combine the sourdough starter, bread flour, warm water, olive oil, and salt. Mix until a shaggy dough forms.
2. Knead the dough on a lightly floured surface for 5-7 minutes, or until smooth and elastic.
3. Place the dough in a greased bowl, cover it with a towel, and let it rise at room temperature for 4-6 hours or until doubled in size.
4. Preheat the oven to 425°F (220°C) and grease a baking sheet.
5. Punch down the risen dough and transfer it to the prepared baking sheet. Press the dough out into a rectangle or circle, about 1/2 inch thick.
6. Drizzle the surface of the dough with olive oil, then sprinkle with minced garlic, chopped rosemary, and coarse sea salt.
7. Bake the focaccia for 20-25 minutes, or until golden brown and crispy on the edges.
8. Allow the focaccia to cool slightly before slicing and serving.

# SOURDOUGH GREEK FLATBREAD (PITA)

**PREP TIME:** Approximately 6-8 hours (including rising time)
**COOK TIME:** 6-8 minutes per batch | **YIELD:** 8 pitas

### INGREDIENTS:

- 1 cup active sourdough starter
- 2 cups all-purpose flour
- 1 teaspoon salt
- 1 tablespoon olive oil
- 3/4 cup warm water
- Additional flour for dusting

### CALORIES: 150 PER SERVING

Total Fat: 1g
Saturated Fat: 0g
Cholesterol: 0mg
Sodium: 300mg
Total Carbohydrate: 30g
Dietary Fiber: 2g
Sugars: 1g
Protein: 5g

### INSTRUCTIONS:

1. In a large mixing bowl, combine the sourdough starter, all-purpose flour, salt, olive oil, and warm water. Mix until a soft dough forms.
2. Turn the dough out onto a lightly floured surface and knead for 5-7 minutes, or until smooth and elastic.
3. Place the dough in a greased bowl, cover it with a towel, and let it rise at room temperature for 6-8 hours or until doubled in size.
4. Preheat the oven to 450°F (230°C) and place a baking stone or upside-down baking sheet inside to preheat.
5. Punch down the risen dough and divide it into 8 equal portions. Shape each portion into a ball.
6. Roll out each ball of dough into a circle, about 1/4 inch thick.
7. Carefully transfer the rolled-out dough circles to the preheated baking stone or baking sheet.
8. Bake the pitas for 3-4 minutes on each side, or until puffed and lightly golden.
9. Remove the pitas from the oven and let them cool slightly before serving.

Mediterranean Inspired

# SOURDOUGH OLIVE BREAD

**PREP TIME:** 7-8 hours (including rising time)
**COOK TIME:** 45-50 minutes per batch | **YIELD:** 1 loaf (approximately 12 servings)

## INGREDIENTS:

- 1 cup active sourdough starter
- 2 cups bread flour
- 1/2 cup whole wheat flour
- 1 teaspoon salt
- 1 cup pitted olives (such as Kalamata or green olives), chopped
- 1 tablespoon olive oil
- 1/4 cup chopped fresh herbs (such as rosemary, thyme, or oregano)

## CALORIES: 160 PER SERVING

Total Fat: 6g
Saturated Fat: 1g
Cholesterol: 0mg
Sodium: 300mg
Total Carbohydrate: 25g
Dietary Fiber: 2g
Sugars: 1g
Protein: 4g

## INSTRUCTIONS:

1. In a large mixing bowl, combine the sourdough starter, bread flour, whole wheat flour, and salt. Mix until a rough dough forms.
2. Add the chopped olives, olive oil, and chopped fresh herbs to the bowl, and knead until well combined.
3. Place the dough in a greased bowl, cover it with a towel, and let it rise at room temperature for 6-8 hours or until doubled in size.
4. Preheat the oven to 450°F (230°C) and place a Dutch oven or baking dish with a lid inside to preheat.
5. Punch down the risen dough and shape it into a round loaf.
6. Carefully transfer the loaf to the preheated Dutch oven or baking dish.
7. Cover the Dutch oven or baking dish with the lid and bake the bread for 30 minutes.
8. Remove the lid and bake for an additional 15-20 minutes, or until the bread is golden brown and sounds hollow when tapped on the bottom.
9. Allow the bread to cool completely before slicing and serving.

# SOURDOUGH MEDITERRANEAN PIZZA

**PREP TIME:** 5-6 hours (including rising time)
**COOK TIME:** 12-15 minutes per batch | **YIELD:** 1 large pizza (approximately 8 slices)

### INGREDIENTS:

- 1 cup active sourdough starter
- 2 cups bread flour
- 1 teaspoon salt
- 1 tablespoon olive oil
- 1/2 cup tomato sauce
- 1 cup mozzarella cheese, shredded
- 1/4 cup sliced black olives
- 1/4 cup chopped sun-dried tomatoes
- 1/4 cup crumbled feta cheese
- Fresh basil leaves for garnish

### INSTRUCTIONS:

1. In a large mixing bowl, combine the active sourdough starter, bread flour, salt, and olive oil. Knead the dough until smooth, then cover and let it rise for 4-6 hours at room temperature.
2. Preheat your oven to 450°F (230°C) and place a pizza stone or baking sheet in the oven to heat up.
3. Roll out the sourdough pizza dough on a floured surface to your desired thickness.
4. Transfer the rolled-out dough to a parchment-lined baking sheet or directly onto the preheated pizza stone.
5. Spread the tomato sauce evenly over the dough, leaving a small border around the edges. Sprinkle the shredded mozzarella cheese over the sauce, then top with sliced black olives, chopped sun-dried tomatoes, and crumbled feta cheese.
6. Bake the pizza in the preheated oven for 12-15 minutes, or until the crust is golden brown and the cheese is bubbly and melted.
7. Remove the pizza from the oven and let it cool slightly before slicing. Garnish with fresh basil leaves and serve hot.

## SOURDOUGH SPANAKOPITA

**PREP TIME:** 7-8 hours (including rising time)
**COOK TIME:** 35-40 minutes | **YIELD:** 12 servings

### INGREDIENTS:

- 1 cup active sourdough starter
- 2 cups all-purpose flour
- 1 teaspoon salt
- 1/4 cup olive oil
- 1/2 cup warm water
- 1 tablespoon olive oil
- 1 small onion, finely chopped
- 2 cloves garlic, minced
- 1 (10-ounce) package frozen chopped spinach, thawed and squeezed dry
- 1/4 cup chopped fresh dill
- 1/4 cup chopped fresh parsley
- 1/4 cup crumbled feta cheese
- Salt and pepper to taste
- 8 sheets phyllo dough
- 1/4 cup melted butter

**CALORIES: 200 PER SERVING**

Total Fat: 10g
Saturated Fat: 5g
Cholesterol: 20mg
Sodium: 350mg
Total Carbohydrate: 20g
Dietary Fiber: 2g
Sugars: 2g
Protein: 6g

### INSTRUCTIONS:

1. In a large mixing bowl, combine the sourdough starter, all-purpose flour, salt, olive oil, and warm water. Mix until a smooth dough forms.

2. Turn the dough out onto a lightly floured surface and knead for 5-7 minutes, or until smooth and elastic.

3. Place the dough in a greased bowl, cover it with a towel, and let it rise at room temperature for 6-8 hours or until doubled in size.

4. While the dough is rising, prepare the filling. Heat 1 tablespoon of olive oil in a skillet over medium heat. Add the chopped onion and garlic and cook until softened, about 5 minutes.

5. Add the thawed and squeezed-dry spinach to the skillet and cook for an additional 2-3 minutes. Remove the skillet from the heat and stir in the chopped fresh dill, chopped fresh parsley, crumbled feta cheese, salt, and pepper.

6. Preheat the oven to 375°F (190°C). Grease a 9x13-inch baking dish.

7. Divide the risen dough into two equal portions. Roll out one portion of dough on a lightly floured surface into a rectangle slightly larger than the baking dish.

8. Carefully transfer the rolled-out dough to the prepared baking dish, pressing it into the bottom and up the sides.

9. Brush the dough with melted butter and place another sheet of phyllo dough on top. Repeat the process until you have used half of the phyllo dough.

10. Spread the spinach and feta cheese filling evenly over the phyllo dough in the baking dish.

11. Continue layering the remaining sheets of phyllo dough on top of the filling, brushing each layer with melted butter.

12. Fold any excess phyllo dough over the top to seal the spanakopita.

13. Bake the spanakopita for 35-40 minutes, or until the phyllo dough is golden brown and crispy.

14. Allow the spanakopita to cool slightly before slicing and serving.

## SOURDOUGH STUFFED GRAPE LEAVES

**PREP TIME:** 8-9 hours (including dough rising time)
**COOK TIME:** 30 minutes | **YIELD:** 24 dolmades (approx. 6 servings)

### INGREDIENTS:

- 1 cup active sourdough starter
- 2 cups all-purpose flour
- 1 teaspoon salt
- 1/2 cup warm water
- 1 tablespoon olive oil
- 1 cup cooked rice
- 1/2 cup finely chopped onion
- 1/4 cup chopped fresh dill
- 1/4 cup chopped fresh parsley
- 2 tablespoons pine nuts
- 2 tablespoons currants
- Salt and pepper to taste
- 1 (8-ounce) jar grape leaves in brine, drained
- Lemon wedges for serving

### CALORIES: 120 PER SERVING

Total Fat: 6g
Saturated Fat: 1g
Cholesterol: 0mg
Sodium: 200mg
Total Carbohydrate: 15g
Dietary Fiber: 1g
Sugars: 0g
Protein: 2g

### INSTRUCTIONS:

1. In a large mixing bowl, combine the sourdough starter, all-purpose flour, salt, olive oil, and warm water. Mix until a smooth dough forms.
2. Turn the dough out onto a lightly floured surface and knead for 5-7 minutes, or until smooth and elastic.
3. Place the dough in a greased bowl, cover it with a towel, and let it rise at room temperature for 6-8 hours or until doubled in size.
4. While the dough is rising, prepare the filling. In a medium mixing bowl, combine the cooked rice, chopped onion, chopped fresh dill, chopped fresh parsley, pine nuts, currants, salt, and pepper. Mix until well combined.

5. Preheat the oven to 350°F (175°C). Grease a baking dish large enough to hold the stuffed grape leaves in a single layer.
6. Lay a grape leaf flat on a clean work surface, shiny side down. Place a small spoonful of the rice filling near the stem end of the leaf.
7. Fold the bottom of the leaf over the filling, then fold in the sides, and roll up tightly into a small bundle.
8. Place the stuffed grape leaves seam side down in the prepared baking dish.
9. Repeat the process with the remaining grape leaves and filling, arranging the stuffed grape leaves in a single layer in the baking dish.
10. Cover the baking dish with foil and bake the stuffed grape leaves for 25-30 minutes, or until heated through.
11. Serve the stuffed grape leaves warm with lemon wedges for squeezing over the top.

# SOURDOUGH MEDITERRANEAN FLATBREAD (LAHMACUN)

**PREP TIME:** 8-9 hours (including dough rising time)
**COOK TIME:** 12 minutes per flatbread | **YIELD:** 4 flatbreads

### INGREDIENTS:

- 1 cup active sourdough starter
- 2 cups all-purpose flour
- 1 teaspoon salt
- 1 tablespoon olive oil
- 3/4 cup warm water
- 1 tablespoon tomato paste
- 2 cloves garlic, minced
- 1 teaspoon ground cumin
- 1 teaspoon paprika
- 1/2 teaspoon ground cinnamon
- 1/2 teaspoon ground allspice
- 1/4 teaspoon cayenne pepper
- 1/2 pound ground lamb or beef
- 1 small onion, finely chopped
- 1 small red bell pepper, finely chopped
- 1 small tomato, finely chopped
- 2 tablespoons chopped fresh parsley
- 2 tablespoons chopped fresh mint
- Salt and pepper to taste
- Lemon wedges for serving

### CALORIES: 250 PER SERVING

Total Fat: 8g
Saturated Fat: 3g
Cholesterol: 20mg
Sodium: 400mg
Total Carbohydrate: 35g
Dietary Fiber: 2g
Sugars: 2g
Protein: 8g

**INSTRUCTIONS:**

1. In a large mixing bowl, combine the sourdough starter, all-purpose flour, salt, olive oil, and warm water. Mix until a smooth dough forms.
2. Turn the dough out onto a lightly floured surface and knead for 5-7 minutes, or until smooth and elastic.
3. Place the dough in a greased bowl, cover it with a towel, and let it rise at room temperature for 6-8 hours or until doubled in size.
4. While the dough is rising, prepare the topping. In a medium mixing bowl, combine the tomato paste, minced garlic, ground cumin, paprika, ground cinnamon, ground allspice, and cayenne pepper. Mix until well combined.
5. Add the ground lamb or beef, chopped onion, chopped red bell pepper, chopped tomato, chopped fresh parsley, chopped fresh mint, salt, and pepper to the bowl. Mix until the ingredients are evenly distributed.
6. Preheat the oven to 450°F (230°C) and place a baking stone or upside-down baking sheet inside to preheat.
7. Divide the risen dough into 4 equal portions. Roll out one portion of dough on a lightly floured surface into a thin circle, about 1/4 inch thick.
8. Place the rolled-out dough on a piece of parchment paper.
9. Spread a thin layer of the prepared topping evenly over the dough, leaving a small border around the edges.
10. Carefully transfer the parchment paper with the topped flatbread to the preheated baking stone or baking sheet.
11. Bake the flatbread for 10-12 minutes, or until the edges are crispy and golden brown.
12. Repeat the process with the remaining portions of dough and topping.
13. Serve the flatbread warm with lemon wedges for squeezing over the top.

# SOURDOUGH OLIVE AND SUN-DRIED TOMATO BREAD

**PREP TIME:** 5-7 hours (including dough rising time)
**COOK TIME:** 25-30 minutes | **YIELD:** 1 loaf

### INGREDIENTS:

- 1 cup active sourdough starter
- 2 cups bread flour
- 1 teaspoon salt
- 1 tablespoon olive oil
- 1/2 cup chopped black olives
- 1/4 cup chopped sun-dried tomatoes (packed in oil)
- 2 tablespoons chopped fresh basil

**CALORIES: APPROXIMATELY 200 PER SERVING**

Total Fat: Approximately 6g
Saturated Fat: Approximately 1g
Cholesterol: Approximately 0mg
Sodium: Approximately 300mg
Total Carbohydrate: Approximately 30g
Dietary Fiber: Approximately 3g
Sugars: Approximately 2g
Protein: Approximately 7g

### INSTRUCTIONS:

1. In a large mixing bowl, combine the active sourdough starter, bread flour, salt, and olive oil. Knead the dough until smooth, then cover and let it rise for 4-6 hours at room temperature.
2. Preheat your oven to 425°F (220°C) and line a baking sheet with parchment paper.
3. Punch down the risen dough and transfer it to the prepared baking sheet. Shape the dough into a loaf, then use a sharp knife to make a few slashes on top.
4. Press chopped black olives, chopped sun-dried tomatoes, and chopped fresh basil into the surface of the dough.
5. Bake the bread in the preheated oven for 25-30 minutes, or until golden brown and cooked through. Let it cool slightly before slicing and serving.
6. These sourdough recipes are inspired by Mediterranean flavors and ingredients, providing a delicious and tangy twist to classic dishes. Enjoy experimenting with these recipes in your kitchen!

# SOURDOUGH SUN-DRIED TOMATO AND BASIL BREAD

**PREP TIME:** 5-8 hours (including dough rising time)
**COOK TIME:** 30-35 minutes | **YIELD:** 1 loaf

## INGREDIENTS:

- 1 cup active sourdough starter
- 3 cups bread flour
- 1 1/4 cups lukewarm water
- 2 tablespoons olive oil
- 2 teaspoons salt
- 1/2 cup sun-dried tomatoes, chopped
- 2 tablespoons fresh basil, chopped

**CALORIES: APPROXIMATELY 210 PER SERVING**

Total Fat: Approximately 5g
Saturated Fat: Approximately 1g
Cholesterol: Approximately 0mg
Sodium: Approximately 400mg
Total Carbohydrate: Approximately 35g
Dietary Fiber: Approximately 2g
Sugars: Approximately 1g
Protein: Approximately 7g

## INSTRUCTIONS:

1. In a large mixing bowl, combine the active sourdough starter, bread flour, lukewarm water, olive oil, and salt. Mix until a shaggy dough forms.
2. Knead the dough for about 5-7 minutes until smooth and elastic.
3. Fold in the chopped sun-dried tomatoes and fresh basil until evenly distributed.
4. Cover the dough and let it rise at room temperature until doubled in size, about 4-6 hours.
5. Shape the dough into a loaf and place it in a lightly greased bread pan. Cover and let rise again for 1-2 hours.
6. Preheat the oven to 375°F (190°C). Slash the top of the risen loaf with a sharp knife.
7. Bake for 30-35 minutes, or until the bread is golden brown and sounds hollow when tapped on the bottom.
8. Let the bread cool on a wire rack before slicing and serving.

# SOURDOUGH MEDITERRANEAN HERB FOUGASSE

**PREP TIME:** 4-6 hours (including dough rising time)
**COOK TIME:** 20-25 minutes | **YIELD:** 1 loaf

### INGREDIENTS:

- 1 cup active sourdough starter
- 3 cups bread flour
- 1 1/4 cups lukewarm water
- 2 tablespoons olive oil
- 2 teaspoons salt
- 2 tablespoons mixed Mediterranean herbs (such as oregano, thyme, and marjoram)

**CALORIES: APPROXIMATELY 190 PER SERVING**

Total Fat: Approximately 4g
Saturated Fat: Approximately 0.5g
Cholesterol: Approximately 0mg
Sodium: Approximately 450mg
Total Carbohydrate: Approximately 32g
Dietary Fiber: Approximately 2g
Sugars: Approximately 1g
Protein: Approximately 6g

### INSTRUCTIONS:

1. Mix the active sourdough starter, bread flour, lukewarm water, olive oil, and salt in a large bowl to form a rough dough.
2. Knead the dough for 8-10 minutes until smooth and elastic.
3. Cover the dough and let it rise until doubled in size, about 4-6 hours.
4. Preheat the oven to 425°F (220°C) and line a baking sheet with parchment paper.
5. Shape the dough into a rough rectangle or oval shape on the prepared baking sheet.
6. Use a sharp knife to slash the dough to create decorative patterns, then sprinkle with mixed Mediterranean herbs.
7. Bake for 20-25 minutes until golden brown and crispy.
8. Allow to cool slightly before serving.

# VEGETARIAN AND VEGAN
## SOURDOUGH RECIPES

Let's delve into the delightful world of vegetarian and vegan sourdough recipes. From hearty breads to flavorful spreads and dips, these recipes are sure to satisfy both your taste buds and your appetite. Let's explore the wonderful possibilities of plant-based sourdough cooking!

List of 10 Vegetarian and Vegan Sourdough Recipes:
1. [Sourdough Avocado Toast](#)
2. [Sourdough Vegan Garlic Bread](#)
3. [Sourdough Vegan Pizza](#)
4. [Sourdough Vegan Bruschetta](#)
5. [Sourdough Vegan Stuffed Mushrooms](#)
6. [Sourdough Vegan Lentil Soup with Sourdough Croutons](#)
7. [Sourdough Vegan Spinach and Artichoke Dip](#)
8. [Sourdough Vegan Falafel](#)
9. [Sourdough Vegan Zucchini Bread](#)
10. [Sourdough Vegan Chocolate Cake](#)

# SOURDOUGH AVOCADO TOAST

**PREP TIME:** 10 minutes | **YIELD:** 2 servings

### INGREDIENTS:

- 2 slices of sourdough bread
- 1 ripe avocado
- 1 tablespoon lemon juice
- Salt and pepper to taste
- Optional toppings: cherry tomatoes, red pepper flakes, microgreens

### CALORIES: 200 PER SERVING

Total Fat: 10g
Saturated Fat: 1.5g
Cholesterol: 0mg
Sodium: 200mg
Total Carbohydrate: 25g
Dietary Fiber: 7g
Sugars: 1g
Protein: 5g

### INSTRUCTIONS:

1. Toast the sourdough bread slices until golden brown.
2. In a small bowl, mash the ripe avocado with lemon juice, salt, and pepper until smooth.
3. Spread the mashed avocado evenly onto the toasted sourdough slices.
4. Top with your favorite toppings such as sliced cherry tomatoes, a sprinkle of red pepper flakes, or a handful of fresh microgreens.
5. Serve immediately and enjoy your delicious sourdough avocado toast!

# SOURDOUGH VEGAN GARLIC BREAD

**PREP TIME:** 10 minutes | **COOK TIME:** 20 minutes | **YIELD:** 8 servings

## INGREDIENTS:

- 1 loaf of sourdough bread
- 1/2 cup vegan butter, softened
- 4 cloves garlic, minced
- 2 tablespoons chopped fresh parsley
- Salt to taste

## CALORIES: 180 PER SERVING

Total Fat: 7g
Saturated Fat: 1g
Cholesterol: 0mg
Sodium: 250mg
Total Carbohydrate: 25g
Dietary Fiber: 2g
Sugars: 1g
Protein: 4g

## INSTRUCTIONS:

1. Preheat the oven to 375°F (190°C).
2. Slice the sourdough bread loaf into thick slices, but do not cut all the way through, leaving the loaf intact at the bottom.
3. In a small bowl, mix together the softened vegan butter, minced garlic, chopped fresh parsley, and salt until well combined.
4. Gently spread the garlic butter mixture between each slice of the sourdough bread, making sure to coat both sides of each slice.
5. Wrap the loaf in aluminum foil and place it on a baking sheet.
6. Bake in the preheated oven for 15-20 minutes, or until the bread is heated through and the garlic butter is melted and fragrant.
7. Remove from the oven, unwrap the foil, and serve the sourdough vegan garlic bread warm. Enjoy the aromatic flavors!

## SOURDOUGH VEGAN PIZZA

**PREP TIME:** 20 minutes | **COOK TIME:** 12-15 minutes | **YIELD:** 1 pizza (8 slices)

### INGREDIENTS:

- 1 batch of sourdough pizza dough
- 1/2 cup tomato sauce
- 1 cup vegan cheese, shredded
- Assorted vegetable toppings (such as bell peppers, onions, mushrooms, olives, etc.)
- Fresh basil leaves for garnish

### CALORIES: 220 PER SERVING

Total Fat: 8g
Saturated Fat: 4g
Cholesterol: 0mg
Sodium: 400mg
Total Carbohydrate: 30g
Dietary Fiber: 3g
Sugars: 2g
Protein: 6g

### INSTRUCTIONS:

1. Preheat the oven to 475°F (245°C).
2. Roll out the sourdough pizza dough on a lightly floured surface to your desired thickness.
3. Transfer the rolled-out dough to a pizza stone or baking sheet lined with parchment paper.
4. Spread the tomato sauce evenly over the pizza dough, leaving a small border around the edges.
5. Sprinkle the shredded vegan cheese over the sauce, then add your favorite vegetable toppings.
6. Place the pizza in the preheated oven and bake for 12-15 minutes, or until the crust is golden brown and the cheese is melted and bubbly.
7. Remove the pizza from the oven and let it cool for a few minutes before slicing.
8. Garnish with fresh basil leaves, slice, and serve your delicious sourdough vegan pizza hot!

# SOURDOUGH VEGAN BRUSCHETTA

**PREP TIME:** 10 minutes | **COOK TIME:** 5-7 minutes | **YIELD:** About 12 slices

## INGREDIENTS:

- 1 baguette or sourdough loaf, sliced
- 4 ripe tomatoes, diced
- 2 cloves garlic, minced
- 2 tablespoons balsamic vinegar
- 2 tablespoons olive oil
- 1/4 cup fresh basil leaves, chopped
- Salt and pepper to taste

**CALORIES: 150 PER SERVING**

Total Fat: 6g
Saturated Fat: 1g
Cholesterol: 0mg
Sodium: 200mg
Total Carbohydrate: 20g
Dietary Fiber: 3g
Sugars: 2g
Protein: 4g

## INSTRUCTIONS:

1. Preheat the oven to 375°F (190°C).
2. Arrange the sliced baguette or sourdough loaf on a baking sheet and toast in the preheated oven for 5-7 minutes, or until lightly golden and crisp.
3. In a mixing bowl, combine the diced tomatoes, minced garlic, balsamic vinegar, olive oil, chopped fresh basil leaves, salt, and pepper. Mix well to combine.
4. Remove the toasted bread slices from the oven and top each slice with a spoonful of the tomato mixture.
5. Serve the sourdough vegan bruschetta immediately as an appetizer or snack. Enjoy the burst of fresh flavors!

# SOURDOUGH VEGAN STUFFED MUSHROOMS

**PREP TIME:** 10 minutes | **COOK TIME:** 15-20 minutes
**YIELD:** 12 servings (one serving per mushroom)

### INGREDIENTS:

- 12 large mushrooms, stems removed
- 1 cup sourdough breadcrumbs
- 1/4 cup vegan cream cheese
- 2 cloves garlic, minced
- 2 tablespoons chopped fresh parsley
- 1 tablespoon olive oil
- Salt and pepper to taste

### CALORIES: 120 PER SERVING

Total Fat: 5g
Saturated Fat: 1g
Cholesterol: 0mg
Sodium: 250mg
Total Carbohydrate: 15g
Dietary Fiber: 3g
Sugars: 2g
Protein: 4g

### INSTRUCTIONS:

1. Preheat the oven to 375°F (190°C).
2. Clean the mushrooms and remove the stems. Set aside.
3. In a mixing bowl, combine the sourdough breadcrumbs, vegan cream cheese, minced garlic, chopped fresh parsley, olive oil, salt, and pepper. Mix until well combined.
4. Stuff each mushroom cap with the breadcrumb mixture, pressing down gently to compact
5. Place the stuffed mushrooms on a baking sheet lined with parchment paper.
6. Bake in the preheated oven for 15-20 minutes, or until the mushrooms are tender and the breadcrumbs are golden brown.
7. Remove from the oven and let cool slightly before serving. Enjoy the savory goodness of these sourdough vegan stuffed mushrooms!

# SOURDOUGH VEGAN LENTIL SOUP WITH SOURDOUGH CROUTONS

**PREP TIME:** 10 minutes | **COOK TIME:** 30-35 minutes | **YIELD:** 4-6 servings

## INGREDIENTS:

- 1 cup dried lentils, rinsed and drained
- 4 cups vegetable broth
- 1 onion, diced
- 2 carrots, diced
- 2 stalks celery, diced
- 3 cloves garlic, minced
- 1 teaspoon ground cumin
- 1 teaspoon ground coriander
- 1/2 teaspoon smoked paprika
- Salt and pepper to taste
- 2 cups sourdough bread, cubed
- 2 tablespoons olive oil
- 2 tablespoons chopped fresh parsley (optional, for garnish)

## CALORIES: 180 PER SERVING

Total Fat: 5g
Saturated Fat: 1g
Cholesterol: 0mg
Sodium: 300mg
Total Carbohydrate: 25g
Dietary Fiber: 6g
Sugars: 3g
Protein: 8g

## INSTRUCTIONS:

1. In a large pot, heat olive oil over medium heat. Add diced onion, carrots, and celery. Cook until vegetables are softened, about 5-7 minutes.
2. Add minced garlic, ground cumin, ground coriander, and smoked paprika. Cook for an additional 1-2 minutes, until fragrant.
3. Add rinsed lentils and vegetable broth to the pot. Bring to a boil, then reduce heat to low and simmer for 20-25 minutes, or until lentils are tender.
4. While the soup is simmering, preheat the oven to 375°F (190°C). Toss cubed sourdough bread with olive oil and spread in a single layer on a baking sheet. Bake for 10-12 minutes, or until crispy and golden brown, to make sourdough croutons.
5. Season the lentil soup with salt and pepper to taste.
6. Serve the soup hot, garnished with sourdough croutons and chopped fresh parsley if desired. Enjoy the comforting flavors of this hearty soup!

Vegetarian and Vegan

# SOURDOUGH VEGAN SPINACH AND ARTICHOKE DIP

**PREP TIME:** 10 minutes | **COOK TIME:** 20-25 minutes
**YIELD:** 6-8 servings (depending on portion size)

## INGREDIENTS:

- 1 cup cooked spinach, chopped
- 1 cup canned artichoke hearts, chopped
- 1 cup vegan cream cheese
- 1/2 cup vegan mayonnaise
- 1/4 cup nutritional yeast
- 2 cloves garlic, minced
- 1 tablespoon lemon juice
- Salt and pepper to taste
- Sourdough bread or tortilla chips, for serving

**CALORIES: 150 PER SERVING**

Total Fat: 8g
Saturated Fat: 1g
Cholesterol: 0mg
Sodium: 250mg
Total Carbohydrate: 15g
Dietary Fiber: 3g
Sugars: 1g
Protein: 6g

## INSTRUCTIONS:

1. Preheat the oven to 375°F (190°C).
2. In a mixing bowl, combine the chopped spinach, chopped artichoke hearts, vegan cream cheese, vegan mayonnaise, nutritional yeast, minced garlic, lemon juice, salt, and pepper. Mix until well combined.
3. Transfer the mixture to a baking dish and spread it out evenly.
4. Bake in the preheated oven for 20-25 minutes, or until bubbly and lightly golden on top.
5. Remove from the oven and let cool slightly before serving.
6. Serve the sourdough vegan spinach and artichoke dip with slices of sourdough bread or tortilla chips. Enjoy the creamy and flavorful dip as a crowd-pleasing appetizer or snack!

# SOURDOUGH VEGAN FALAFEL

**PREP TIME:** 10 minutes (if chickpeas are already cooked
**COOK TIME:** 3-4 minutes per side (frying time may vary depending on pan size and heat)
**YIELD:** 6-8 falafels (depending on size)

## INGREDIENTS:

- 1 cup cooked chickpeas
- 1/2 cup chopped fresh parsley
- 1/4 cup chopped fresh cilantro
- 1/4 cup chopped onion
- 2 cloves garlic, minced
- 2 tablespoons all-purpose flour
- 1 tablespoon lemon juice
- 1 teaspoon ground cumin
- 1 teaspoon ground coriander
- 1/2 teaspoon baking powder
- Salt and pepper to taste
- Olive oil for frying

## CALORIES: 180 PER SERVING

Total Fat: 8g
Saturated Fat: 1g
Cholesterol: 0mg
Sodium: 350mg
Total Carbohydrate: 20g
Dietary Fiber: 5g
Sugars: 2g
Protein: 6g

## INSTRUCTIONS:

1. In a food processor, combine cooked chickpeas, chopped fresh parsley, chopped fresh cilantro, chopped onion, minced garlic, all-purpose flour, lemon juice, ground cumin, ground coriander, baking powder, salt, and pepper.
2. Pulse the mixture until it forms a coarse paste.
3. Shape the mixture into small patties or balls.
4. Heat olive oil in a skillet over medium heat.
5. Fry the falafel patties in batches until golden brown and crispy on both sides, about 3-4 minutes per side.
6. Remove falafel from the skillet and place on a plate lined with paper towels to drain excess oil.
7. Serve the sourdough vegan falafel hot, with your favorite sauces, salads, or in pita bread as sandwiches. Enjoy the flavorful and satisfying falafel as a delicious vegetarian meal!

# SOURDOUGH VEGAN ZUCCHINI BREAD

**PREP TIME:** 10 minutes | **COOK TIME:** 50-60 minutes | **YIELD:** 8-10 slices

## INGREDIENTS:

- 2 cups shredded zucchini
- 1/2 cup mashed ripe banana
- 1/2 cup unsweetened applesauce
- 1/4 cup maple syrup
- 1/4 cup coconut oil, melted
- 2 teaspoons vanilla extract
- 2 cups all-purpose flour
- 1 teaspoon baking powder
- 1/2 teaspoon baking soda
- 1/2 teaspoon salt
- 1 teaspoon ground cinnamon
- 1/4 teaspoon ground nutmeg
- 1/4 cup chopped walnuts or pecans (optional)

## CALORIES: 160 PER SERVING

Total Fat: 6g
Saturated Fat: 1g
Cholesterol: 0mg
Sodium: 200mg
Total Carbohydrate: 25g
Dietary Fiber: 3g
Sugars: 10g
Protein: 4g

## INSTRUCTIONS:

1. Preheat the oven to 350°F (175°C). Grease a 9x5-inch loaf pan or line with parchment paper.
2. In a large mixing bowl, combine shredded zucchini, mashed ripe banana, unsweetened applesauce, maple syrup, melted coconut oil, and vanilla extract. Mix until well combined.
3. In a separate bowl, whisk together all-purpose flour, baking powder, baking soda, salt, ground cinnamon, and ground nutmeg.
4. Add the dry ingredients to the wet ingredients and stir until just combined. Fold in chopped walnuts or pecans if using.
5. Pour the batter into the prepared loaf pan and spread it out evenly.
6. Bake in the preheated oven for 50-60 minutes, or until a toothpick inserted into the center comes out clean.
7. Remove from the oven and let the bread cool in the pan for 10 minutes before transferring to a wire rack to cool completely.
8. Slice and serve the sourdough vegan zucchini bread as a tasty breakfast treat or afternoon snack. Enjoy the moist and flavorful bread bursting with zucchini goodness!

# SOURDOUGH VEGAN CHOCOLATE CAKE

**PREP TIME:** 10 minutes | **COOK TIME:** 25-30 minutes | **YIELD:** 8 slices

## INGREDIENTS:

- 1 1/2 cups all-purpose flour
- 1 cup granulated sugar
- 1/4 cup unsweetened cocoa powder
- 1 teaspoon baking soda
- 1/2 teaspoon salt
- 1 cup water
- 1/3 cup vegetable oil
- 1 tablespoon white vinegar
- 1 teaspoon vanilla extract
- Vegan chocolate frosting (store-bought or homemade)

### CALORIES: 200 PER SERVING

Total Fat: 10g
Saturated Fat: 2g
Cholesterol: 0mg
Sodium: 250mg
Total Carbohydrate: 30g
Dietary Fiber: 3g
Sugars: 15g
Protein: 4g

## INSTRUCTIONS:

1. Preheat the oven to 350°F (175°C). Grease and flour a 9-inch round cake pan or line it with parchment paper.
2. In a large mixing bowl, sift together all-purpose flour, granulated sugar, cocoa powder, baking soda, and salt.
3. In a separate bowl, whisk together water, vegetable oil, white vinegar, and vanilla extract.
4. Pour the wet ingredients into the dry ingredients and stir until just combined. Be careful not to overmix.
5. Pour the batter into the prepared cake pan and spread it out evenly.
6. Bake in the preheated oven for 25-30 minutes, or until a toothpick inserted into the center comes out clean.
7. Remove the cake from the oven and let it cool in the pan for 10 minutes before transferring it to a wire rack to cool completely.
8. Once the cake has cooled completely, frost it with vegan chocolate frosting.

Vegetarian and Vegan

9. Slice and serve the sourdough vegan chocolate cake as a decadent dessert for any occasion. Enjoy the rich and moist cake with its deep chocolate flavor!

With these ten delightful recipes, you have a plethora of options to explore the world of vegetarian and vegan sourdough cooking. From savory appetizers like garlic bread and stuffed mushrooms to comforting dishes like lentil soup and chocolate cake, each recipe is crafted to tantalize your taste buds and nourish your body. Get creative in the kitchen and experiment with different flavors and ingredients to make these recipes your own. Whether you're hosting a dinner party, enjoying a cozy night in, or simply treating yourself to something special, these sourdough creations are sure to impress. So gather your ingredients, roll up your sleeves, and let the culinary adventure begin!

# HEALTH-CONSCIOUS CREATIONS

Welcome to delectable sourdough recipes crafted with health-conscious eaters in mind. In this section, we'll explore ten nutritious and flavorful dishes that prioritize wholesome ingredients without compromising on taste. From hearty breads to satisfying meals and snacks, these recipes are designed to nourish your body and delight your taste buds. Let's dive into the world of health-conscious sourdough creations!

List of Health-Concious Sourdough Recipes:
1. Sourdough Multigrain Bread
2. Sourdough Chia Seed Crackers
3. Sourdough Sweet Potato Pancakes
4. Sourdough Vegan Lentil Soup with Sourdough Croutons
5. Sourdough Veggie Buddha Bowl with Turmeric Tahini Dressing
6. Sourdough Chia Seed Pudding Parfait
7. Sourdough Spinach and Feta Stuffed Portobello Mushrooms

# SOURDOUGH MULTIGRAIN BREAD

**PREP TIME:** 10 minutes | **COOK TIME:** 1 hour 10 minutes (includes rising times) | **YIELD:** 1 loaf

### INGREDIENTS:

- 1 cup active sourdough starter
- 2 cups bread flour
- 1/2 cup whole wheat flour
- 1/2 cup rye flour
- 1/4 cup rolled oats
- 1/4 cup flax seeds
- 2 tablespoons honey or maple syrup
- 1 1/4 cups warm water
- 2 teaspoons salt

### CALORIES: 150 PER SERVING

Total Fat: 2g
Saturated Fat: 0.5g
Cholesterol: 0mg
Sodium: 200mg
Total Carbohydrate: 30g
Dietary Fiber: 5g
Sugars: 2g
Protein: 6g

### INSTRUCTIONS:

1. In a large mixing bowl, combine the active sourdough starter, bread flour, whole wheat flour, rye flour, rolled oats, flaxseeds, honey or maple syrup, and warm water.
2. Mix until a shaggy dough forms, then knead on a lightly floured surface for 8-10 minutes, until smooth and elastic.
3. Place the dough in a greased bowl, cover with a clean towel, and let it rise at room temperature for 4-6 hours, or until doubled in size.
4. Punch down the risen dough and shape it into a loaf.
5. Place the shaped dough in a greased loaf pan, cover, and let it rise for another 1-2 hours, until it fills the pan.
6. Preheat the oven to 375°F (190°C). Slash the top of the risen dough with a sharp knife, then bake in the preheated oven for 35-40 minutes, or until golden brown and hollow-sounding when tapped on the bottom.
7. Remove from the oven and let the bread cool completely on a wire rack before slicing. Enjoy slices of this wholesome multigrain sourdough bread with your favorite toppings!

# SOURDOUGH CHIA SEED CRACKERS

**PREP TIME:** 10 minutes | **COOK TIME:** 15-20 minutes | **YIELD:** 20-25 crackers

## INGREDIENTS:

- 1 cup sourdough discard
- 1/2 cup whole wheat flour
- 1/4 cup chia seeds
- 1/4 cup sesame seeds
- 1/4 cup sunflower seeds
- 1/4 cup pumpkin seeds
- 1/4 cup water
- 2 tablespoons olive oil
- 1 teaspoon salt
- 1/2 teaspoon garlic powder
- 1/2 teaspoon onion powder

## CALORIES: 120 PER SERVING

Total Fat: 6g
Saturated Fat: 1g
Cholesterol: 0mg
Sodium: 150mg
Total Carbohydrate: 15g
Dietary Fiber: 3g
Sugars: 0g
Protein: 4g

## INSTRUCTIONS:

1. In a large mixing bowl, combine the sourdough discard, whole wheat flour, chia seeds, sesame seeds, sunflower seeds, pumpkin seeds, water, olive oil, salt, garlic powder, and onion powder.
2. Mix until a dough forms, then knead on a lightly floured surface for a few minutes until smooth.
3. Divide the dough into two equal portions and roll out each portion thinly between two sheets of parchment paper.
4. Use a pizza cutter or knife to cut the rolled-out dough into desired cracker shapes.
5. Transfer the cut crackers, still on parchment paper, to baking sheets.
6. Bake in a preheated oven at 350°F (175°C) for 15-20 minutes, or until golden brown and crispy.
7. Remove from the oven and let the sourdough chia seed crackers cool completely before breaking them apart along the scored lines.
8. Store in an airtight container at room temperature for up to a week. Enjoy these crunchy and nutritious crackers as a wholesome snack!

# SOURDOUGH SWEET POTATO PANCAKES

**PREP TIME:** 10 minutes | **COOK TIME:** 5-7 minutes per side
**YIELD:** 2-3 pancakes (depending on size)

### INGREDIENTS:

- 1 cup sourdough starter
- 1 cup cooked and mashed sweet potato
- 2 eggs
- 1/4 cup milk (dairy or plant-based)
- 2 tablespoons maple syrup
- 1 teaspoon vanilla extract
- 1 cup whole wheat flour
- 1 teaspoon baking powder
- 1/2 teaspoon baking soda
- 1/2 teaspoon ground cinnamon
- 1/4 teaspoon ground nutmeg
- Pinch of salt
- Butter or oil for cooking

### CALORIES: 180 PER SERVING

Total Fat: 5g
Saturated Fat: 1g
Cholesterol: 20mg
Sodium: 250mg
Total Carbohydrate: 30g
Dietary Fiber: 3g
Sugars: 5g
Protein: 6g

### INSTRUCTIONS:

1. In a large mixing bowl, combine the sourdough starter, mashed sweet potato, eggs, milk, maple syrup, and vanilla extract.
2. In a separate bowl, whisk together the whole wheat flour, baking powder, baking soda, ground cinnamon, ground nutmeg, and salt.
3. Gradually add the dry ingredients to the wet ingredients, stirring until just combined. Be careful not to overmix.
4. Heat a skillet or griddle over medium heat and grease with butter or oil.
5. Pour the pancake batter onto the skillet, using about 1/4 cup for each pancake.
6. Cook until bubbles form on the surface of the pancakes, then flip and cook until golden brown on the other side.
7. Repeat with the remaining batter, greasing the skillet as needed.
8. Serve the sourdough sweet potato

# SOURDOUGH VEGAN LENTIL SOUP WITH SOURDOUGH CROUTONS

**PREP TIME:** 10 minutes | **COOK TIME:** 30-35 minutes | **YIELD:** 4-6 servings

## INGREDIENTS:

- 1 cup dried lentils, rinsed and drained
- 4 cups vegetable broth
- 1 onion, diced
- 2 carrots, diced
- 2 stalks celery, diced
- 3 cloves garlic, minced
- 1 teaspoon ground cumin
- 1 teaspoon ground coriander
- 1/2 teaspoon smoked paprika
- Salt and pepper to taste
- 2 cups sourdough bread, cubed
- 2 tablespoons olive oil
- 2 tablespoons chopped fresh parsley (optional, for garnish)

## CALORIES: 220 PER SERVING

Total Fat: 5g
Saturated Fat: 1g
Cholesterol: 0mg
Sodium: 400mg
Total Carbohydrate: 35g
Dietary Fiber: 8g
Sugars: 5g
Protein: 10g

## INSTRUCTIONS:

1. In a large pot, heat olive oil over medium heat. Add diced onion, carrots, and celery. Cook until vegetables are softened, about 5-7 minutes.
2. Add minced garlic, ground cumin, ground coriander, and smoked paprika. Cook for an additional 1-2 minutes, until fragrant.
3. Add rinsed lentils and vegetable broth to the pot. Bring to a boil, then reduce heat to low and simmer for 20-25 minutes, or until lentils are tender.

4. While the soup is simmering, preheat the oven to 375°F (190°C). Toss cubed sourdough bread with olive oil and spread in a single layer on a baking sheet. Bake for 10-12 minutes, or until crispy and golden brown, to make sourdough croutons.
5. Season the lentil soup with salt and pepper to taste.
6. Serve the soup hot, garnished with sourdough croutons and chopped fresh parsley if desired. Enjoy the comforting flavors of this hearty soup!

# SOURDOUGH VEGGIE BUDDHA BOWL WITH TURMERIC TAHINI DRESSING

**INGREDIENTS:**

- 1 cup cooked quinoa
- 1 cup roasted sweet potatoes, cubed
- 1 cup steamed broccoli florets
- 1 cup shredded red cabbage
- 1/2 cup sliced avocado
- 1/4 cup sliced radishes
- 1/4 cup sliced cucumber
- 2 tablespoons chopped fresh cilantro (optional, for garnish)
- 2 tablespoons sesame seeds (optional, for garnish)
- Turmeric Tahini Dressing
- 1/4 cup tahini
- 2 tablespoons lemon juice
- 1 tablespoon maple syrup
- 1 teaspoon ground turmeric
- 1/2 teaspoon ground cumin
- Salt and pepper to taste
- Water (as needed for consistency)

**CALORIES: 250 PER SERVING**

Total Fat: 12g
Saturated Fat: 2g
Cholesterol: 0mg
Sodium: 350mg
Total Carbohydrate: 30g
Dietary Fiber: 8g
Sugars: 5g
Protein: 9g

Health Conscious Creations

**INSTRUCTIONS:**

1. In a small bowl, whisk together all the ingredients for the turmeric tahini dressing until smooth. Add water as needed to reach your desired consistency. Set aside.
2. Assemble the buddha bowls by dividing cooked quinoa, roasted sweet potatoes, steamed broccoli, shredded red cabbage, sliced avocado, sliced radishes, and sliced cucumber among serving bowls.
3. Drizzle the turmeric tahini dressing over the buddha bowls.
4. Garnish with chopped fresh cilantro and sesame seeds, if desired.
5. Serve the sourdough veggie buddha bowls immediately and enjoy a wholesome and nutritious meal packed with vibrant flavors!

# SOURDOUGH CHIA SEED PUDDING PARFAIT

**PREP TIME:** 10 minutes | **COOK TIME:** N/A (requires chilling) | **YIELD:** 1 serving

## INGREDIENTS:

- 1/4 cup chia seeds
- 1 cup unsweetened almond milk
- 1 tablespoon maple syrup or honey
- 1/2 teaspoon vanilla extract
- 1/2 cup Greek yogurt or coconut yogurt
- 1/2 cup mixed berries (such as strawberries, blueberries, raspberries)
- 1/4 cup granola
- Sliced bananas (optional, for garnish)
- Sourdough croutons (optional, for crunch)

**CALORIES: 180 PER SERVING**

Total Fat: 8g
Saturated Fat: 1g
Cholesterol: 0mg
Sodium: 150mg
Total Carbohydrate: 20g
Dietary Fiber: 7g
Sugars: 6g
Protein: 5g

## INSTRUCTIONS:

1. In a bowl, mix chia seeds, almond milk, maple syrup or honey, and vanilla extract. Stir well to combine.
2. Cover the bowl and refrigerate for at least 2 hours or overnight, until the chia pudding thickens.
3. Once the chia pudding has set, layer it with Greek yogurt or coconut yogurt in serving glasses or bowls.
4. Top with mixed berries, granola, sliced bananas, and sourdough croutons for added texture.
5. Serve the sourdough chia seed pudding parfait immediately or refrigerate until ready to enjoy. Indulge in a nutritious and satisfying treat that's perfect for breakfast or as a healthy snack!

# SOURDOUGH SPINACH AND FETA STUFFED PORTOBELLO MUSHROOMS

**PREP TIME:** 10 minutes | **COOK TIME:** 15-20 minutes | **YIELD:** 4 serving

## INGREDIENTS:

- 4 large portobello mushrooms, stems removed
- 2 cups fresh spinach, chopped
- 1/2 cup crumbled feta cheese
- 2 cloves garlic, minced
- 1 tablespoon olive oil
- Salt and pepper to taste
- Sourdough breadcrumbs (for topping)

**CALORIES: 150 PER SERVING**

Total Fat: 8g
Saturated Fat: 3g
Cholesterol: 20mg
Sodium: 300mg
Total Carbohydrate: 12g
Dietary Fiber: 4g
Sugars: 3g
Protein: 9g

## INSTRUCTIONS:

1. Preheat the oven to 375°F (190°C). Line a baking sheet with parchment paper.
2. Place portobello mushrooms on the prepared baking sheet, gill side up.
3. In a skillet, heat olive oil over medium heat. Add minced garlic and chopped spinach. Cook until spinach wilts, about 2-3 minutes.
4. Remove skillet from heat and stir in crumbled feta cheese. Season with salt and pepper to taste.
5. Spoon the spinach and feta mixture into the cavity of each portobello mushroom.
6. Sprinkle sourdough breadcrumbs over the stuffed mushrooms.
7. Bake in the preheated oven for 15-20 minutes, or until mushrooms

**SOURDOUGH**
ASIAN FUSION

In this mouth-watering chapter, we'll embark on a flavorful journey blending the ancient tradition of sourdough with the vibrant and diverse flavors of Asian cuisine. From savory dumplings to sweet treats, these recipes offer a unique twist on classic Asian dishes, infused with the tangy goodness of sourdough. Get ready to tantalize your taste buds with these delightful creations!

List of 10 Asian inspired Sourdough Recipes:
1. Sourdough Kimchi Pancakes
2. Sourdough Steamed Bao Buns
3. Sourdough Scallion Pancakes
4. Sourdough Veggie Spring Rolls with Peanut Dipping Sauce
5. Sourdough Teriyaki Tofu Stir-Fry
6. Sourdough Matcha Swirl Bread
7. Sourdough Coconut Curry Soup
8. Sourdough Char Siu Pork Buns
9. Sourdough Korean BBQ Beef Tacos
10. Sourdough Mango Sticky Rice

Get ready to dive into a fusion of flavors as we explore each of these unique sourdough recipes inspired by Asian cuisine. Let's get cooking!

# SOURDOUGH KIMCHI PANCAKES

**PREP TIME:** 10 minutes | **COOK TIME:** 2-3 minutes per side
**YIELD:** about 6-8 pancakes (depending on size)

### INGREDIENTS:

- 1 cup sourdough starter
- 1 cup kimchi, chopped
- 1/4 cup kimchi juice
- 1/2 cup all-purpose flour
- 2 tablespoons soy sauce
- 2 green onions, chopped
- 2 tablespoons vegetable oil

### CALORIES: 180 PER SERVING

Total Fat: 6g
Saturated Fat: 1g
Cholesterol: 0mg
Sodium: 350mg
Total Carbohydrate: 25g
Dietary Fiber: 2g
Sugars: 1g
Protein: 5g

### INSTRUCTIONS:

1. In a large mixing bowl, combine the sourdough starter, chopped kimchi, kimchi juice, all-purpose flour, soy sauce, and chopped green onions. Mix until well combined.
2. Heat vegetable oil in a non-stick skillet over medium heat.
3. Pour a ladleful of the pancake batter into the skillet and spread it out into a thin pancake.
4. Cook for 2-3 minutes on each side, or until golden brown and crispy.
5. Repeat with the remaining batter.
6. Serve the sourdough kimchi pancakes hot, with dipping sauce if desired.

# SOURDOUGH STEAMED BAO BUNS

**PREP TIME:** 10 minutes | **COOK TIME:** 10-12 minutes
**YIELD:** Makes buns to be filled (quantity not specified)

### INGREDIENTS:

- 1 cup sourdough starter
- 2 cups all-purpose flour
- 1/4 cup warm water
- 1 tablespoon sugar
- 1 teaspoon active dry yeast
- 1/2 teaspoon baking powder
- Pinch of salt
- 1 tablespoon vegetable oil

### CALORIES: 150 PER SERVING

Total Fat: 2g
Saturated Fat: 0g
Cholesterol: 0mg
Sodium: 300mg
Total Carbohydrate: 30g
Dietary Fiber: 1g
Sugars: 1g
Protein: 5g

### INSTRUCTIONS:

1. In a mixing bowl, combine the sourdough starter, all-purpose flour, warm water, sugar, and active dry yeast. Mix until a dough forms.
2. Knead the dough on a floured surface for 5-7 minutes, or until smooth and elastic.
3. Place the dough in a greased bowl, cover with a clean kitchen towel, and let it rise in a warm place for 1-2 hours, or until doubled in size.
4. Punch down the dough and knead in the baking powder and salt.
5. Divide the dough into small balls and roll each ball into a flat circle.
6. Place the dough circles on individual squares of parchment paper and brush the tops with vegetable oil.
7. Fold each circle in half to form a semi-circle and place them in a steamer basket lined with parchment paper.
8. Steam the buns for 10-12 minutes, or until puffed up and cooked through.
9. Serve the sourdough steamed bao buns filled with your favorite fillings, such as barbecue pork, tofu, or vegetables.

Sourdough Asian Fusion | 135

## SOURDOUGH SCALLION PANCAKES

**PREP TIME:** 10 minutes | **COOK TIME:** 2-3 minutes per side
**YIELD:** about 6-8 pancakes (depending on size)

### INGREDIENTS:

- 1 cup sourdough starter
- 1 cup all-purpose flour
- 1/2 cup warm water
- 2 tablespoons vegetable oil
- 1/2 cup chopped scallions
- Salt to taste
- Additional vegetable oil for frying

Calories: 160 per serving
Total Fat: 4g
Saturated Fat: 0.5g
Cholesterol: 0mg
Sodium: 300mg
Total Carbohydrate: 25g
Dietary Fiber: 2g
Sugars: 1g
Protein: 5g

### INSTRUCTIONS:

1. In a mixing bowl, combine the sourdough starter, all-purpose flour, warm water, and vegetable oil. Mix until a smooth batter forms.
2. Stir in the chopped scallions and season with salt to taste.
3. Heat vegetable oil in a non-stick skillet over medium heat.
4. Pour a ladleful of the pancake batter into the skillet and spread it out into a thin pancake.
5. Cook for 2-3 minutes on each side, or until golden brown and crispy.
6. Repeat with the remaining batter, adding more oil to the skillet as needed.
7. Serve the sourdough scallion pancakes hot, with soy sauce or dipping sauce if desired.

# SOURDOUGH **VEGGIE SPRING ROLLS** WITH **PEANUT DIPPING SAUCE**

**PREP TIME:** 10 minutes
**COOK TIME:** Depends on cooking time of vermicelli noodles (usually 3-5 minutes)
**YIELD:** 8 veggie spring rolls

### INGREDIENTS:

- 8 spring roll wrappers
- 1 cup cooked vermicelli noodles
- 1 cup shredded lettuce
- 1 cup shredded carrots
- 1 cup shredded cucumber
- 1/2 cup fresh cilantro leaves
- 1/4 cup chopped peanuts (for garnish)
- Sourdough starter discard (optional, for added flavor)

For Peanut Dipping Sauce:
- 1/4 cup creamy peanut butter
- 2 tablespoons soy sauce
- 1 tablespoon maple syrup
- 1 tablespoon rice vinegar
- 1 clove garlic, minced
- 1 teaspoon grated fresh ginger
- 2-4 tablespoons warm water (as needed to thin out the sauce)

### CALORIES: 120 PER SERVING

Total Fat: 4g
Saturated Fat: 1g
Cholesterol: 0mg
Sodium: 200mg
Total Carbohydrate: 20g
Dietary Fiber: 3g
Sugars: 3g
Protein: 4g

Sourdough Asian Fusion

**INSTRUCTIONS:**

1. Prepare the peanut dipping sauce by combining peanut butter, soy sauce, maple syrup, rice vinegar, minced garlic, and grated ginger in a bowl. Mix well, then gradually add warm water until the sauce reaches your desired consistency. Set aside.
2. Place a spring roll wrapper on a clean surface.
3. Arrange a small portion of cooked vermicelli noodles, shredded lettuce, shredded carrots, shredded cucumber, and cilantro leaves in the center of the wrapper.
4. Optionally, add a tablespoon of sourdough starter discard for added flavor.
5. Fold the bottom of the wrapper over the filling, then fold the sides towards the center, and roll tightly to seal.
6. Repeat with the remaining wrappers and filling ingredients.
7. Serve the sourdough veggie spring rolls with the peanut dipping sauce, garnished with chopped peanuts.
8. Enjoy these fresh and flavorful spring rolls as a light and healthy appetizer or snack!

# SOURDOUGH TERIYAKI TOFU STIR-FRY

**PREP TIME:** 10 minutes (includes marinating time) | **COOK TIME:** 10-12 minutes
**YIELD:** 1-2 people

### INGREDIENTS:

- 1 block (14 oz) firm tofu, drained and cubed
- 2 tablespoons soy sauce
- 2 tablespoons teriyaki sauce
- 1 tablespoon rice vinegar
- 1 tablespoon maple syrup
- 2 cloves garlic, minced
- 1 teaspoon grated fresh ginger
- 2 tablespoons vegetable oil
- 1 bell pepper, sliced
- 1 cup broccoli florets
- Cooked rice, for serving

### CALORIES: 220 PER SERVING

Total Fat: 8g
Saturated Fat: 1g
Cholesterol: 0mg
Sodium: 400mg
Total Carbohydrate: 30g
Dietary Fiber: 4g
Sugars: 8g
Protein: 10g

### INSTRUCTIONS:

1. In a bowl, combine soy sauce, teriyaki sauce, rice vinegar, maple syrup, minced garlic, and grated ginger to make the marinade.
2. Add cubed tofu to the marinade and let it marinate for at least 15 minutes.
3. Heat vegetable oil in a large skillet or wok over medium-high heat.
4. Add marinated tofu cubes (reserving the marinade) to the skillet and cook until browned and crispy on all sides, about 5-7 minutes. Remove tofu from the skillet and set aside.
5. In the same skillet, add sliced bell pepper and broccoli florets. Cook until vegetables are tender-crisp, about 4-5 minutes.
6. Return tofu to the skillet, along with the reserved marinade. Cook for an additional 2-3 minutes, until heated through and the sauce has thickened slightly.
7. Serve the sourdough teriyaki tofu stir-fry over cooked rice. Enjoy this flavorful and satisfying dish!

# SOURDOUGH MATCHA SWIRL BREAD

**PREP TIME:** 10 minutes | **COOK TIME:** 30-35 minutes | **YIELD:** 1 loaf

## INGREDIENTS:

- 1 cup sourdough starter
- 2 cups all-purpose flour
- 1/2 cup warm water
- 2 tablespoons sugar
- 1 tablespoon matcha green tea powder
- 1 teaspoon active dry yeast
- 1/2 teaspoon salt
- 1 tablespoon vegetable oil

## CALORIES: 190 PER SERVING

Total Fat: 6g
Saturated Fat: 1.5g
Cholesterol: 0mg
Sodium: 250mg
Total Carbohydrate: 30g
Dietary Fiber: 1g
Sugars: 10g
Protein: 4g

## INSTRUCTIONS:

1. In a mixing bowl, combine sourdough starter, all-purpose flour, warm water, sugar, matcha powder, active dry yeast, and salt. Mix until a dough forms.
2. Knead the dough on a floured surface for 5-7 minutes, or until smooth and elastic.
3. Place the dough in a greased bowl, cover with a clean kitchen towel, and let it rise in a warm place for 1-2 hours, or until doubled in size.
4. Punch down the dough and shape it into a rectangle.
5. Roll the dough into a log, then twist it to create a swirl pattern.
6. Place the dough in a greased loaf pan, cover, and let it rise for another 30-45 minutes.
7. Preheat the oven to 375°F (190°C).
8. Bake the sourdough matcha swirl bread in the preheated oven for 30-35 minutes, or until golden brown and hollow-sounding when tapped on the bottom.
9. Let the bread cool in the pan for 10 minutes before transferring it to a wire rack to cool completely.
10. Slice and serve the sourdough matcha swirl bread with butter or your favorite spreads. Enjoy this unique and visually stunning bread!

# SOURDOUGH COCONUT CURRY SOUP

**PREP TIME:** 10 minutes | **COOK TIME:** 20-25 minutes
**YIELD:** 6-8 servings (depending on portion size)

## INGREDIENTS:

- 1 tablespoon vegetable oil
- 1 onion, diced
- 2 cloves garlic, minced
- 1 tablespoon grated fresh ginger
- 2 tablespoons curry powder
- 1 can (14 oz) coconut milk
- 4 cups vegetable broth
- 2 cups chopped vegetables (such as carrots, bell peppers, and broccoli)
- 1 cup cooked chickpeas
- 1 cup cooked rice or noodles
- Salt and pepper to taste
- Fresh cilantro for garnish

## CALORIES: 180 PER SERVING

Total Fat: 10g
Saturated Fat: 8g
Cholesterol: 0mg
Sodium: 400mg
Total Carbohydrate: 20g
Dietary Fiber: 3g
Sugars: 5g
Protein: 3g

## INSTRUCTIONS:

1. Heat vegetable oil in a large pot over medium heat.
2. Add diced onion, minced garlic, and grated ginger to the pot. Cook until onions are translucent and fragrant, about 3-4 minutes.
3. Stir in curry powder and cook for an additional 1-2 minutes.
4. Pour in coconut milk and vegetable broth. Bring to a simmer.
5. Add chopped vegetables and cooked chickpeas to the pot. Cook until vegetables are tender, about 10-15 minutes.
6. Stir in cooked rice or noodles and simmer for an additional 5 minutes.
7. Season with salt and pepper to taste.
8. Ladle the sourdough coconut curry soup into bowls and garnish with fresh cilantro.
9. Serve hot and enjoy the comforting flavors of this delicious soup!

# SOURDOUGH CHAR SIU PORK BUNS

**PREP TIME:** 2 hours 10 minutes (includes marinating time)
**COOK TIME:** 40-45 minutes | **YIELD:** 8-10 buns (depending on size)

## INGREDIENTS:

For the Char Siu Pork:
- 1 lb pork shoulder, thinly sliced
- 2 cloves garlic, minced
- 2 tablespoons hoisin sauce
- 2 tablespoons soy sauce
- 1 tablespoon honey
- 1 tablespoon Chinese rice wine (or dry sherry)
- 1 tablespoon sesame oil
- 1 teaspoon five-spice powder
- 1/2 teaspoon ground white pepper

For the Buns:
- 1 cup sourdough starter
- 2 cups all-purpose flour
- 1/4 cup warm water
- 2 tablespoons sugar
- 1 teaspoon baking powder
- 1/4 teaspoon baking soda
- Pinch of salt
- Vegetable oil, for greasing

**CALORIES: 240 PER SERVING**

Total Fat: 6g
Saturated Fat: 2g
Cholesterol: 25mg
Sodium: 450mg
Total Carbohydrate: 35g
Dietary Fiber: 1g
Sugars: 10g
Protein: 10g

## INSTRUCTIONS:

For the Char Siu Pork:

1. In a bowl, combine minced garlic, hoisin sauce, soy sauce, honey, rice wine, sesame oil, five-spice powder, and ground white pepper to make the marinade.

2. Add thinly sliced pork shoulder to the marinade, ensuring it's well coated. Marinate for at least 2 hours or overnight in the refrigerator.
3. Preheat the oven to 375°F (190°C). Place the marinated pork on a baking sheet lined with parchment paper.
4. Roast in the preheated oven for 20-25 minutes, or until the pork is cooked through and caramelized. Remove from the oven and let it cool slightly before slicing.

For the Buns:

1. In a mixing bowl, combine sourdough starter, all-purpose flour, warm water, sugar, baking powder, baking soda, and a pinch of salt. Mix until a dough forms.
2. Knead the dough on a floured surface for 5-7 minutes, or until smooth and elastic.
3. Place the dough in a greased bowl, cover with a clean kitchen towel, and let it rise in a warm place for 1-2 hours, or until doubled in size.
4. Punch down the dough and divide it into equal-sized portions. Roll each portion into a ball and flatten into a circle.
5. Place a slice of char siu pork in the center of each dough circle, then gather the edges and pinch to seal, forming a bun.
6. Place the buns on a parchment-lined baking sheet, cover, and let them rise for another 30-45 minutes.
7. Preheat the oven to 375°F (190°C). Brush the tops of the buns with vegetable oil.
8. Bake in the preheated oven for 15-20 minutes, or until golden brown.
9. Serve the sourdough char siu pork buns hot, as a delicious appetizer or snack.

# SOURDOUGH KOREAN BBQ BEEF TACOS

**PREP TIME:** 2 hours 10 minutes (includes marinating time)
**COOK TIME:** 20-25 minutes | **YIELD:** 8 tacos (depending on size)

### INGREDIENTS:

For the Korean BBQ Beef:
- 1 lb beef sirloin, thinly sliced
- 3 tablespoons soy sauce
- 2 tablespoons brown sugar
- 2 tablespoons sesame oil
- 2 cloves garlic, minced
- 1 teaspoon grated fresh ginger
- 1 tablespoon rice vinegar
- 1 tablespoon gochujang (Korean chili paste)
- 2 green onions, chopped (for garnish)
- Sesame seeds (for garnish)

For the Tacos:
- 8 small flour tortillas
- 1 cup sourdough starter
- 2 cups all-purpose flour
- 1/4 cup warm water
- 1 teaspoon baking powder
- 1/4 teaspoon baking soda
- Pinch of salt
- Vegetable oil, for greasing

### CALORIES: 280 PER SERVING

Total Fat: 12g
Saturated Fat: 4g
Cholesterol: 30mg
Sodium: 500mg
Total Carbohydrate: 30g
Dietary Fiber: 3g
Sugars: 5g
Protein: 15g

## INSTRUCTIONS:

### For the Korean BBQ Beef:

1. In a bowl, combine soy sauce, brown sugar, sesame oil, minced garlic, grated ginger, rice vinegar, and gochujang to make the marinade.
2. Add thinly sliced beef sirloin to the marinade, ensuring it's well coated. Marinate for at least 2 hours or overnight in the refrigerator.
3. Heat a skillet or grill pan over medium-high heat. Cook the marinated beef slices for 2-3 minutes on each side, or until cooked through and caramelized.
4. Remove from heat and sprinkle with chopped green onions and sesame seeds.

### For the Tacos:

1. In a mixing bowl, combine sourdough starter, all-purpose flour, warm water, baking powder, baking soda, and a pinch of salt. Mix until a dough forms.
2. Knead the dough on a floured surface for 5-7 minutes, or until smooth and elastic.
3. Divide the dough into equal-sized portions. Roll each portion into a ball and flatten into a circle.
4. Heat a lightly greased skillet over medium heat. Cook the tortillas for 1-2 minutes on each side, or until lightly browned and puffed.
5. Assemble the tacos by placing a spoonful of Korean BBQ beef onto each tortilla. Garnish with additional chopped green onions and sesame seeds if desired.

## SOURDOUGH MANGO STICKY RICE

**PREP TIME:** 10 minutes | **COOK TIME:** 23-25 minutes | **YIELD:** 2-3 servings

### INGREDIENTS:

- 1 cup glutinous rice (sticky rice)
- 1 cup coconut milk
- 1/4 cup sugar
- 1/4 teaspoon salt
- 2 ripe mangoes, peeled and sliced
- Sourdough starter discard (optional, for added flavor)

### CALORIES: 250 PER SERVING

Total Fat: 2g
Saturated Fat: 0.5g
Cholesterol: 0mg
Sodium: 10mg
Total Carbohydrate: 55g
Dietary Fiber: 3g
Sugars: 25g
Protein: 4g

### INSTRUCTIONS:

1. Rinse the glutinous rice under cold water until the water runs clear. Drain well.
2. In a saucepan, combine glutinous rice, coconut milk, sugar, salt, and sourdough starter discard (if using). Stir to combine.
3. Bring the mixture to a boil over medium-high heat, then reduce heat to low. Cover and simmer for 18-20 minutes, or until the rice is tender and the liquid is absorbed.
4. Remove from heat and let the rice sit, covered, for 5 minutes.
5. Fluff the cooked rice with a fork and let it cool slightly.
6. Serve the sourdough mango sticky rice warm or at room temperature, topped with sliced ripe mangoes.
7. Enjoy this delightful and tropical dessert!

SOURDOUGH **LATIN AMERICAN** FLAVORS

Get ready to spice up your kitchen with a fusion of sourdough and Latin American cuisine! From savory empanadas to sweet churros, these recipes will transport you to the vibrant streets of Latin America with every bite. Let's dive into these delightful creations:

List of 10 Latin American Sourdough Recipes:
1. Sourdough Arepas with Avocado Salsa
2. Sourdough Empanadas filled with Beef and Potatoes
3. Sourdough Tostadas with Black Bean Salsa
4. Sourdough Pupusas stuffed with Cheese and Beans
5. Sourdough Chicken Tortilla Soup
6. Sourdough Plantain Chips with Guacamole
7. Sourdough Cilantro Lime Rice
8. Sourdough Carnitas Tacos with Pineapple Salsa
9. Sourdough Enchiladas with Red Sauce
10. Sourdough Churros with Chocolate Dipping Sauce

Get ready to embark on a culinary journey filled with bold flavors and exciting twists on traditional Latin American dishes. Let's dive into these mouthwatering recipes!

Absolutely! Let's dive into each of these flavorful sourdough recipes:

# SOURDOUGH AREPAS WITH AVOCADO SALSA

**PREP TIME:** 15 minutes (including salsa prep)
**COOK TIME:** 10-12 minutes (5-6 minutes per side for arepas)
**YIELD:** 8 tacos (depending on size)

## INGREDIENTS:

For the Arepas:
- 1 cup sourdough starter
- 1 cup pre-cooked white cornmeal (masarepa)
- 1 cup warm water
- 1 teaspoon salt
- 2 tablespoons vegetable oil

For the Avocado Salsa:
- 2 ripe avocados, diced
- 1 tomato, diced
- 1/4 cup red onion, finely chopped
- 1/4 cup cilantro, chopped
- 1 jalapeño, seeded and minced
- Juice of 1 lime
- Salt and pepper to taste

**CALORIES: 200 PER SERVING**

Total Fat: 8g
Saturated Fat: 1.5g
Cholesterol: 0mg
Sodium: 300mg
Total Carbohydrate: 30g
Dietary Fiber: 3g
Sugars: 1g
Protein: 5g

## INSTRUCTIONS:

1. In a mixing bowl, combine the sourdough starter, pre-cooked white cornmeal, warm water, and salt. Mix until a dough forms.
2. Divide the dough into equal portions and shape each portion into a round disc, about 1/2 inch thick.
3. Heat vegetable oil in a skillet over medium heat. Cook the arepas for 5-6 minutes on each side, or until golden brown and cooked through.
4. Meanwhile, prepare the avocado salsa by combining diced avocados, tomato, red onion, cilantro, jalapeño, lime juice, salt, and pepper in a bowl. Mix well.
5. Serve the warm sourdough arepas with the avocado salsa on top. Enjoy this delightful Latin American treat!

# SOURDOUGH EMPANADAS FILLED WITH BEEF AND POTATOES

**PREP TIME:** 45 minutes (including resting time for dough)
**COOK TIME:** 30-35 minutes (sautéing, baking)
**YIELD:** Makes 10-12 empanadas (depending on size)

### INGREDIENTS:

For the Empanada Dough:
- 1 cup sourdough starter
- 2 cups all-purpose flour
- 1/2 cup warm water
- 1/4 cup vegetable oil
- 1 teaspoon salt

For the Filling:
- 1 lb ground beef
- 2 potatoes, diced
- 1 onion, chopped
- 2 cloves garlic, minced
- 1 teaspoon ground cumin
- 1 teaspoon paprika
- Salt and pepper to taste
- Vegetable oil for frying

**CALORIES: 220 PER SERVING**

Total Fat: 10g
Saturated Fat: 4g
Cholesterol: 30mg
Sodium: 350mg
Total Carbohydrate: 25g
Dietary Fiber: 2g
Sugars: 1g
Protein: 8g

### INSTRUCTIONS:

1. In a mixing bowl, combine sourdough starter, all-purpose flour, warm water, vegetable oil, and salt. Knead until a smooth dough forms. Cover and let it rest for 30 minutes.
2. In a skillet, heat vegetable oil over medium heat. Add chopped onion and minced garlic, and sauté until softened.

Sourdough Latin Amaerican Flavors

3. Add ground beef to the skillet and cook until browned. Stir in diced potatoes, ground cumin, paprika, salt, and pepper. Cook until potatoes are tender. Remove from heat and let it cool.
4. Preheat the oven to 375°F (190°C).
5. Roll out the dough on a floured surface and cut into circles using a round cutter.
6. Place a spoonful of the beef and potato filling in the center of each dough circle. Fold the dough over the filling to form a half-moon shape and seal the edges by crimping with a fork.
7. Place the empanadas on a baking sheet lined with parchment paper. Bake in the preheated oven for 20-25 minutes, or until golden brown.
8. Serve the sourdough empanadas hot, with salsa or chimichurri sauce for dipping. Enjoy this classic Latin American dish!

# SOURDOUGH TOSTADAS WITH BLACK BEAN SALSA

**PREP TIME:** 30 minutes (including resting time for dough)
**COOK TIME:** 15-20 minutes (frying tortillas, salsa prep)
**YIELD:** Makes 4 tostadas

### INGREDIENTS:

For the Tostadas:
- 4 small corn tortillas
- 1 cup sourdough starter
- 2 cups all-purpose flour
- 1/4 cup warm water
- 1 teaspoon baking powder
- 1/4 teaspoon salt
- Vegetable oil for frying

For the Black Bean Salsa:
- 1 can (15 oz) black beans, drained and rinsed
- 1 tomato, diced
- 1/4 cup red onion, finely chopped
- 1/4 cup cilantro, chopped
- 1 jalapeño, seeded and minced
- Juice of 1 lime
- Salt and pepper to taste

### CALORIES: 180 PER SERVING

Total Fat: 6g
Saturated Fat: 1g
Cholesterol: 0mg
Sodium: 250mg
Total Carbohydrate: 25g
Dietary Fiber: 5g
Sugars: 2g
Protein: 6g

### INSTRUCTIONS:

1. In a mixing bowl, combine sourdough starter, all-purpose flour, warm water, baking powder, and salt. Mix until a dough forms. Cover and let it rest for 30 minutes.

2. Roll out the dough on a floured surface and cut into circles using a round cutter.
3. Heat vegetable oil in a skillet over medium-high heat. Fry the tortillas until golden brown and crispy. Remove from the oil and drain on paper towels.
4. In a separate bowl, combine drained black beans, diced tomato, chopped red onion, chopped cilantro, minced jalapeño, lime juice, salt, and pepper to make the salsa. Mix well.
5. Spread a spoonful of the black bean salsa on each fried tortilla to make the tostadas.
6. Serve the sourdough tostadas with additional toppings such as avocado slices, shredded lettuce, or sour cream if desired. Enjoy this crunchy and flavorful dish!

# SOURDOUGH PUPUSAS STUFFED WITH CHEESE AND BEANS

**PREP TIME:** 30 minutes (including resting time for dough)
**COOK TIME:** 6-8 minutes (frying pupusas)
**YIELD:** Makes 8-10 pupusas (depending on size)

## INGREDIENTS:

For the Pupusa Dough:
- 1 cup sourdough starter
- 2 cups masa harina
- 1 1/4 cups warm water
- 1/2 teaspoon salt
- Vegetable oil for cooking

For the Filling:
- 1 cup refried black beans
- 1 cup shredded cheese (such as mozzarella or Monterey Jack)

**CALORIES: 160 PER SERVING**

Total Fat: 6g
Saturated Fat: 3g
Cholesterol: 15mg
Sodium: 300mg
Total Carbohydrate: 20g
Dietary Fiber: 3g
Sugars: 1g
Protein: 6g

## INSTRUCTIONS:

1. In a mixing bowl, combine sourdough starter, masa harina, warm water, and salt. Knead until a smooth dough forms. Cover and let it rest for 30 minutes.
2. Divide the dough into equal-sized portions and flatten each portion into a circle.
3. Place a spoonful of refried black beans and shredded cheese in the center of each dough circle.
4. Fold the dough over the filling to enclose it completely, then flatten the pupusa to about 1/4 inch thickness.
5. Heat vegetable oil in a skillet over medium heat. Cook the pupusas for 3-4 minutes on each side, or until golden brown and cooked through.
6. Serve the sourdough pupusas hot, topped with curtido (pickled cabbage slaw) and salsa roja (red salsa). Enjoy this traditional Salvadoran dish!

Sourdough Latin Amaerican Flavors

# SOURDOUGH CHICKEN TORTILLA SOUP

**PREP TIME:** 30 minutes (including resting time for dough)
**COOK TIME:** 6-8 minutes (frying pupusas)  |  **YIELD:** Makes 8-10 pupusas (depending on size)

### INGREDIENTS:

- 2 tablespoons vegetable oil
- 1 onion, diced
- 2 cloves garlic, minced
- 1 jalapeño pepper, seeded and diced
- 1 red bell pepper, diced
- 1 green bell pepper, diced
- 1 teaspoon ground cumin
- 1 teaspoon chili powder
- 1 teaspoon paprika
- 1 can (14 oz) diced tomatoes
- 4 cups chicken broth
- 2 cups cooked shredded chicken
- 1 cup corn kernels (fresh, frozen, or canned)
- 1 cup black beans, drained and rinsed
- Salt and pepper to taste
- Sourdough bread for serving

### CALORIES: 220 PER SERVING

Total Fat: 10g
Saturated Fat: 2g
Cholesterol: 40mg
Sodium: 500mg
Total Carbohydrate: 20g
Dietary Fiber: 3g
Sugars: 4g
Protein: 12g

### INSTRUCTIONS:

1. In a large pot, heat vegetable oil over medium heat. Add diced onion, minced garlic, diced jalapeño pepper, diced red bell pepper, and diced green bell pepper. Sauté until vegetables are softened, about 5-7 minutes.
2. Stir in ground cumin, chili powder, and paprika. Cook for an additional 2 minutes until fragrant.
3. Add diced tomatoes (with their juices) and chicken broth to the pot. Bring to a simmer.
4. Stir in cooked shredded chicken, corn kernels, and black beans. Simmer for 15-20 minutes to allow the flavors to meld together.
5. Season with salt and pepper to taste.
6. Serve the sourdough chicken tortilla soup hot, garnished with tortilla strips, avocado slices, shredded cheese, cilantro, and a wedge of lime. Enjoy the comforting flavors of this hearty soup!

# SOURDOUGH PLANTAIN CHIPS WITH GUACAMOLE

**PREP TIME:** 20 minutes (including prep for both)
**COOK TIME:** 15-20 minutes (baking plantain chips) | **YIELD:** depending on portion size

## INGREDIENTS:

For the Plantain Chips:

- 2 ripe plantains
- 2 tablespoons vegetable oil
- Salt to taste

For the Guacamole:

- 2 ripe avocados
- 1 tomato, diced
- 1/4 cup diced red onion
- 1 jalapeño pepper, seeded and minced
- Juice of 1 lime
- Salt and pepper to taste
- Fresh cilantro for garnish

**CALORIES: 180 PER SERVING**

Total Fat: 10g
Saturated Fat: 2g
Cholesterol: 0mg
Sodium: 250mg
Total Carbohydrate: 25g
Dietary Fiber: 4g
Sugars: 6g
Protein: 2g

## INSTRUCTIONS:

For the Plantain Chips:

1. Preheat the oven to 400°F (200°C).
2. Peel the plantains and slice them thinly using a mandoline slicer or a sharp knife.
3. In a bowl, toss the plantain slices with vegetable oil until evenly coated.
4. Place the plantain slices on a baking sheet lined with parchment paper in a single layer, ensuring they are not touching each other.
5. Bake in the preheated oven for 15-20 minutes, flipping halfway through, or until golden brown and crispy.
6. Remove from the oven and sprinkle with salt to taste.

For the Guacamole:

1. In a bowl, mash the ripe avocados with a fork until smooth.
2. Stir in diced tomato, diced red onion, minced jalapeño pepper, and lime juice.
3. Season with salt and pepper to taste.
4. Garnish with fresh cilantro.
5. Serve the sourdough plantain chips with guacamole for a delicious and addictive snack that's perfect for parties or game nights!

# SOURDOUGH CARNITAS TACOS WITH PINEAPPLE SALSA

**PREP TIME:** 15 minutes | **COOK TIME:** 2-3 hours | **YIELD:** 4-6 people

### INGREDIENTS:

For the Carnitas:

- 1 lb pork shoulder, cut into chunks
- 1 onion, quartered
- 4 cloves garlic, smashed
- 1 orange, juiced
- 1 lime, juiced
- 1 teaspoon ground cumin
- 1 teaspoon dried oregano
- 1 teaspoon smoked paprika
- Salt and pepper to taste
- 1 tablespoon vegetable oil

For the Pineapple Salsa:

- 1 cup diced fresh pineapple
- 1/4 cup diced red onion
- 1 jalapeño pepper, seeded and diced
- Juice of 1 lime
- 2 tablespoons chopped fresh cilantro
- Salt to taste

For Serving:

- Sourdough tortillas
- Additional toppings such as diced avocado, shredded cabbage, and sour cream

### CALORIES: 250 PER SERVING

Total Fat: 12g
Saturated Fat: 3g
Cholesterol: 30mg
Sodium: 350mg
Total Carbohydrate: 25g
Dietary Fiber: 3g
Sugars: 4g
Protein: 12g

Sourdough Latin Amaerican Flavors

## INSTRUCTIONS:

### For the Carnitas:

1. Season pork shoulder chunks generously with salt and pepper.
2. In a large skillet or Dutch oven, heat vegetable oil over medium-high heat. Add seasoned pork shoulder chunks and sear until browned on all sides.
3. Add quartered onion, smashed garlic cloves, orange juice, lime juice, ground cumin, dried oregano, and smoked paprika to the skillet.
4. Bring to a simmer, then reduce heat to low. Cover and cook for 2-3 hours, or until the pork is tender and easily shreds with a fork.
5. Once cooked, remove the pork from the skillet and shred it using two forks.
6. Heat a separate skillet over medium-high heat. Add shredded pork in batches and cook until crispy and caramelized.

### For the Pineapple Salsa:

1. In a bowl, combine diced fresh pineapple, diced red onion, diced jalapeño pepper, lime juice, chopped fresh cilantro, and salt to taste. Mix well.

### For Serving:

1. Warm sourdough tortillas on a skillet or in the microwave.
2. Fill each tortilla with crispy carnitas and top with pineapple salsa and additional toppings as desired.
3. Serve the sourdough carnitas tacos hot, with lime wedges on the side.

# SOURDOUGH ENCHILADAS WITH RED SAUCE

**PREP TIME:** 20 minutes | **COOK TIME:** 20-25 minutes | **YIELD:** 4-6 people

## INGREDIENTS:

For the Red Sauce:

- 2 tablespoons vegetable oil
- 2 tablespoons all-purpose flour
- 2 tablespoons chili powder
- 1 teaspoon ground cumin
- 1/2 teaspoon garlic powder
- 1/4 teaspoon dried oregano
- 2 cups chicken or vegetable broth
- 1 can (8 oz) tomato sauce
- Salt to taste

For the Enchiladas:

- 8 sourdough tortillas
- 2 cups cooked shredded chicken or cooked black beans for a vegetarian option
- 1 cup shredded cheese (cheddar, Monterey Jack, or a blend)
- Chopped fresh cilantro for garnish
- Sour cream and diced avocado for serving

**CALORIES: 280 PER SERVING**

Total Fat: 14g
Saturated Fat: 5g
Cholesterol: 40mg
Sodium: 500mg
Total Carbohydrate: 25g
Dietary Fiber: 3g
Sugars: 5g
Protein: 14g

## INSTRUCTIONS:

For the Red Sauce:

1. In a saucepan, heat vegetable oil over medium heat. Stir in all-purpose flour and cook for 1 minute, stirring constantly.
2. Add chili powder, ground cumin, garlic powder, and dried oregano to the saucepan. Cook for an additional minute, stirring constantly.

3. Gradually whisk in chicken or vegetable broth and tomato sauce until smooth.
4. Bring to a simmer and cook for 10-15 minutes, stirring occasionally, until the sauce thickens.
5. Season with salt to taste.

**For the Enchiladas:**
1. Preheat the oven to 350°F (175°C). Grease a baking dish.
2. Warm sourdough tortillas on a skillet or in the microwave to make them pliable.
3. Spoon a portion of cooked shredded chicken or black beans onto each tortilla, then sprinkle with shredded cheese.
4. Roll up the tortillas tightly and place them seam side down in the prepared baking dish.
5. Pour the red sauce over the rolled-up tortillas, spreading it evenly.
6. Sprinkle additional shredded cheese over the top of the enchiladas.
7. Bake in the preheated oven for 20-25 minutes, or until the cheese is melted and bubbly.
8. Garnish with chopped fresh cilantro.
9. Serve the sourdough enchiladas hot, with sour cream and diced avocado on the side.

# SOURDOUGH CHURROS WITH CHOCOLATE DIPPING SAUCE

**PREP TIME:** 10 minutes | **COOK TIME:** 5-7 minutes | **YIELD:** About 12 churros

## INGREDIENTS:

For the Churros:
- 1 cup water
- 2 tablespoons sugar
- 1/2 teaspoon salt
- 2 tablespoons vegetable oil
- 1 cup all-purpose flour
- 1/4 cup sourdough starter
- Vegetable oil for frying

For the Chocolate Dipping Sauce:
- 1/2 cup heavy cream
- 4 oz dark chocolate, chopped
- 1 tablespoon unsalted butter
- 1/2 teaspoon vanilla extract

**CALORIES: 220 PER SERVING**

Total Fat: 10g
Saturated Fat: 6g
Cholesterol: 20mg
Sodium: 150mg
Total Carbohydrate: 30g
Dietary Fiber: 1g
Sugars: 15g
Protein: 3g

## INSTRUCTIONS:

For the Churros:

1. In a saucepan, combine water, sugar, salt, and vegetable oil. Bring to a boil over medium heat.
2. Remove from heat and stir in all-purpose flour and sourdough starter until a smooth dough forms.
3. Transfer the dough to a piping bag fitted with a star tip.
4. Heat vegetable oil in a deep skillet or pot to 375°F (190°C).

Sourdough Latin Amaerican Flavors

5. Pipe strips of dough directly into the hot oil, using scissors to cut them to desired lengths.
6. Fry the churros until golden brown and crispy, about 2-3 minutes per side.
7. Remove the fried churros from the oil and drain on paper towels to remove excess oil.

**For the Chocolate Dipping Sauce:**
1. In a small saucepan, heat heavy cream until simmering.
2. Remove from heat and stir in chopped dark chocolate until melted and smooth.
3. Stir in unsalted butter and vanilla extract until well combined.
4. Pour the chocolate dipping sauce into a serving bowl.

Serve the sourdough churros warm, dusted with powdered sugar and accompanied by the chocolate dipping sauce.

# SOURDOUGH **HOLIDAY** SPECIALS

List of 10 Holiday Special Sourdough Recipes:
1. Sourdough Cranberry Walnut Bread
2. Sourdough Pumpkin Spice Bread
3. Sourdough Eggnog Pancakes
4. Sourdough Gingerbread Cookies
5. Sourdough Stuffing
6. Sourdough Holiday Bread Pudding with Bourbon Sauce
7. Sourdough Holiday Wreath Bread
8. Sourdough Holiday Stollen
9. Sourdough Apple Cider Donuts
10. Sourdough Holiday Buche de Noel (Yule Log)

# SOURDOUGH CRANBERRY WALNUT BREAD

**PREP TIME:** 10 minutes | **COOK TIME:** 1 hour 5-20 minutes (includes rise time)
**YIELD:** 1 round loaf (about 8-10 slices)

### INGREDIENTS:

- 300g active sourdough starter
- 400g bread flour
- 100g whole wheat flour
- 10g salt
- 250g water
- 100g dried cranberries
- 75g chopped walnuts

### NUTRITION FACTS: (PER SERVING)

- Calories: 220
- Total Fat: 4g
- Saturated Fat: 0.5g
- Cholesterol: 0mg
- Sodium: 370mg
- Total Carbohydrate: 40g
- Dietary Fiber: 3g
- Sugars: 8g
- Protein: 6g

(Note: Nutrition facts are approximate and may vary based on specific ingredients used.)

### INSTRUCTIONS:

1. In a large bowl, mix together the active sourdough starter, bread flour, whole wheat flour, salt, and water until a shaggy dough forms.
2. Knead the dough for about 10 minutes until smooth and elastic.
3. Fold in the dried cranberries and chopped walnuts until evenly distributed.
4. Cover the bowl and let the dough rise at room temperature for 6-8 hours or until doubled in size.
5. Preheat the oven to 450°F (230°C) with a Dutch oven inside.
6. Transfer the risen dough to a lightly floured surface and shape it into a round loaf.
7. Carefully place the loaf into the preheated Dutch oven, cover with the lid, and bake for 30 minutes.
8. Remove the lid and bake for an additional 15-20 minutes until the crust is golden brown.
9. Let the bread cool completely before slicing and serving.

# SOURDOUGH PUMPKIN SPICE BREAD

**PREP TIME:** 10 minutes | **COOK TIME:** 1 hour 5-20 minutes (includes rise time)
**YIELD:** 1 round loaf (about 8-10 slices)

### INGREDIENTS:

- 300g active sourdough starter
- 400g bread flour
- 100g whole wheat flour
- 10g salt
- 250g water
- 200g canned pumpkin puree
- 100g granulated sugar
- 2 teaspoons pumpkin pie spice

### NUTRITION FACTS: (PER SERVING)

- Calories: 200
- Total Fat: 1g
- Saturated Fat: 0g
- Cholesterol: 0mg
- Sodium: 370mg
- Total Carbohydrate: 42g
- Dietary Fiber: 2g
- Sugars: 7g
- Protein: 5g

### INSTRUCTIONS:

1. Follow the same instructions as the Sourdough Cranberry Walnut Bread, but fold in the pumpkin puree, granulated sugar, and pumpkin pie spice instead of cranberries and walnuts.

# SOURDOUGH EGGNOG PANCAKES

**PREP TIME:** 10 minutes
**COOK TIME:** 15-20 minutes (depending on size and number of pancakes cooked at once)
**YIELD:** About 8 pancakes

### INGREDIENTS:

- 200g sourdough starter
- 150g all-purpose flour
- 1 cup eggnog
- 1 egg
- 2 tablespoons melted butter
- 2 tablespoons granulated sugar
- 1 teaspoon baking powder
- 1/2 teaspoon baking soda
- 1/2 teaspoon ground nutmeg
- Butter or oil for cooking

### NUTRITION FACTS:
(per serving, makes about 8 pancakes)

- Calories: 180
- Total Fat: 7g
- Saturated Fat: 4g
- Cholesterol: 45mg
- Sodium: 250mg
- Total Carbohydrate: 25g
- Dietary Fiber: 1g
- Sugars: 6g
- Protein: 5g

### INSTRUCTIONS:

1. In a large bowl, mix together the sourdough starter, all-purpose flour, eggnog, egg, melted butter, and granulated sugar until well combined.
2. Add the baking powder, baking soda, and ground nutmeg to the batter and stir until just combined.
3. Heat a lightly greased skillet or griddle over medium heat.
4. Pour 1/4 cup of batter onto the skillet for each pancake.
5. Cook until bubbles form on the surface of the pancakes, then flip and cook until golden brown on the other side.
6. Serve warm with maple syrup and additional nutmeg if desired.

# SOURDOUGH GINGERBREAD COOKIES

**PREP TIME:** 15 minutes (including chilling time)
**COOK TIME:** 10-12 minutes | **YIELD:** About 24 cookies

## INGREDIENTS:

- 200g active sourdough starter
- 150g all-purpose flour
- 50g whole wheat flour
- 100g unsalted butter, softened
- 100g brown sugar
- 1 egg
- 2 tablespoons molasses
- 1 teaspoon ground ginger
- 1/2 teaspoon ground cinnamon
- 1/4 teaspoon ground cloves
- 1/4 teaspoon ground nutmeg
- 1/4 teaspoon salt

## NUTRITION FACTS:
(per serving, makes about 24 cookies)

- Calories: 90
- Total Fat: 4g
- Saturated Fat: 2.5g
- Cholesterol: 20mg
- Sodium: 50mg
- Total Carbohydrate: 12g
- Dietary Fiber: 0.5g
- Sugars: 6g
- Protein: 1g

## INSTRUCTIONS:

1. In a mixing bowl, cream together the softened butter and brown sugar until light and fluffy.
2. Add the egg and molasses, and mix until well combined.
3. Stir in the active sourdough starter until fully incorporated.
4. In a separate bowl, whisk together the all-purpose flour, whole wheat flour, ground ginger, ground cinnamon, ground cloves, ground nutmeg, and salt.
5. Gradually add the dry ingredients to the wet ingredients, mixing until a dough forms.
6. Wrap the dough in plastic wrap and refrigerate for at least 1 hour.

7. Preheat the oven to 350°F (175°C) and line a baking sheet with parchment paper.
8. Roll out the chilled dough on a floured surface to about 1/4 inch thickness.
9. Use cookie cutters to cut out desired shapes and place them on the prepared baking sheet.
10. Bake for 10-12 minutes, or until the edges are lightly browned.
11. Let the cookies cool on the baking sheet for a few minutes before transferring them to a wire rack to cool completely.
12. Decorate with icing or enjoy as is!

# SOURDOUGH STUFFING

**PREP TIME:** 10 minutes | **COOK TIME:** 40-45 minutes | **YIELD:** About 8 servings

## INGREDIENTS:

- 400g sourdough bread, cubed and dried
- 2 tablespoons unsalted butter
- 1 onion, chopped
- 2 celery stalks, chopped
- 2 cloves garlic, minced
- 1 teaspoon dried sage
- 1 teaspoon dried thyme
- 1/2 teaspoon dried rosemary
- 1/2 teaspoon salt
- 1/4 teaspoon black pepper
- 2 cups chicken or vegetable broth
- 1/4 cup chopped fresh parsley

## NUTRITION FACTS:
(per serving, makes about 8 servings)

- Calories: 160
- Total Fat: 4g
- Saturated Fat: 2g
- Cholesterol: 10mg
- Sodium: 450mg
- Total Carbohydrate: 25g
- Dietary Fiber: 2g
- Sugars: 3g
- Protein: 5g

## INSTRUCTIONS:

1. Preheat the oven to 350°F (175°C) and grease a baking dish.
2. In a large skillet, melt the butter over medium heat.
3. Add the chopped onion and celery to the skillet and cook until softened, about 5 minutes.
4. Add the minced garlic, dried sage, dried thyme, dried rosemary, salt, and black pepper to the skillet and cook for an additional 1-2 minutes, until fragrant.
5. In a large bowl, combine the dried sourdough bread cubes with the cooked vegetable mixture.
6. Pour the chicken or vegetable broth over the bread mixture and toss until well combined.
7. Transfer the mixture to the prepared baking dish and cover with foil.
8. Bake for 25 minutes, then remove the foil and bake for an additional 10-15 minutes, until the top is golden brown.
9. Sprinkle with chopped fresh parsley before serving.

## SOURDOUGH HOLIDAY BREAD PUDDING

**PREP TIME:** 10 minutes | **COOK TIME:** 40-45 minutes | **YIELD:** About 8 servings

### INGREDIENTS:

- 8 cups cubed sourdough bread
- 4 large eggs
- 2 cups whole milk
- 1/2 cup granulated sugar
- 1/4 cup unsalted butter, melted
- 1 teaspoon vanilla extract
- 1/2 teaspoon ground cinnamon
- 1/4 teaspoon ground nutmeg
- 1/4 teaspoon salt
- 1 cup dried cranberries
- 1/2 cup chopped pecans
- Powdered sugar, for dusting (optional)
- Whipped cream or vanilla ice cream, for serving (optional)

### NUTRITION FACTS:

Calories: 450
Total Fat: 20g
Saturated Fat: 8g
Cholesterol: 125mg
Sodium: 300mg
Total Carbohydrate: 60g
Dietary Fiber: 3g
Sugars: 30g
Protein: 10g

### INSTRUCTIONS:

1. Preheat the oven to 350°F (175°C) and grease a 9x13-inch baking dish.
2. In a large bowl, whisk together the eggs, whole milk, granulated sugar, melted butter, vanilla extract, ground cinnamon, ground nutmeg, and salt until well combined.
3. Add the cubed sourdough bread, dried cranberries, and chopped pecans to the egg mixture. Stir until the bread is evenly coated.
4. Pour the bread pudding mixture into the prepared baking dish, spreading it out evenly.
5. Bake for 40-45 minutes, or until the top is golden brown and the pudding is set.
6. Let the bread pudding cool slightly before serving.
7. Dust with powdered sugar if desired, and serve warm with whipped cream or vanilla ice cream.
8. Nutrition Facts: (per serving, makes about 8 servings)

# SOURDOUGH HOLIDAY WREATH BREAD

**PREP TIME:** 30 minutes (including rising time)
**COOK TIME:** 1-2 hours (includes rising time) | **YIELD:** About 12 servings

## INGREDIENTS:

For the dough:
- 300g active sourdough starter
- 500g bread flour
- 250ml lukewarm water
- 50g granulated sugar
- 100g unsalted butter, softened
- 2 large eggs
- 1 teaspoon salt

For the filling:
- 1/2 cup granulated sugar
- 2 tablespoons ground cinnamon
- 1/2 cup chopped nuts (such as walnuts or pecans)
- 1/2 cup dried fruit (such as raisins or cranberries)

For the glaze:
- 1 cup powdered sugar
- 2-3 tablespoons milk
- 1/2 teaspoon vanilla extract

## NUTRITION FACTS:
(per serving, makes about 12 servings)

Calories: 300
Total Fat: 10g
Saturated Fat: 5g
Cholesterol: 45mg
Sodium: 200mg
Total Carbohydrate: 48g
Dietary Fiber: 2g
Sugars: 20g
Protein: 6g

## INSTRUCTIONS:

1. In a large mixing bowl, combine the active sourdough starter, bread flour, lukewarm water, granulated sugar, softened butter, eggs, and salt. Mix until a dough forms.

2. Knead the dough for about 10 minutes until smooth and elastic.

3. Cover the bowl and let the dough rise at room temperature for 2-3 hours, or until doubled in size.

Sourdough Holiday Specials

4. Punch down the dough and roll it out into a large rectangle on a floured surface.
5. In a small bowl, mix together the granulated sugar and ground cinnamon for the filling.
6. Spread the softened butter evenly over the dough, then sprinkle the filling mixture evenly over the buttered surface of the dough, followed by the chopped nuts and dried fruit.
7. Starting from one long edge, tightly roll up the dough into a log. Once rolled, pinch the seam to seal.
8. Using a sharp knife, carefully slice the log in half lengthwise, leaving about 1 inch at the top end uncut. Twist the two halves together, forming a braided rope.
9. Shape the twisted dough into a circle and pinch the ends together to seal, forming a wreath shape. Transfer the wreath to a parchment-lined baking sheet.
10. Cover the wreath loosely with plastic wrap and let it rise for an additional 1-2 hours, or until puffy.
11. Preheat the oven to 350°F (175°C).
12. Once risen, bake the wreath in the preheated oven for 25-30 minutes, or until golden brown and cooked through.
13. While the wreath is baking, prepare the glaze by whisking together the powdered sugar, milk, and vanilla extract until smooth.
14. Once the wreath is done baking, remove it from the oven and let it cool for a few minutes on the baking sheet.
15. Drizzle the glaze over the warm wreath, then slice and serve.

# SOURDOUGH HOLIDAY STOLLEN

**PREP TIME:** 30 minutes (including rising time)
**COOK TIME:** 1-2 hours (includes rising time) | **YIELD:** About 12 servings

## INGREDIENTS:

For the dough:

- 300g active sourdough starter
- 500g bread flour
- 150ml lukewarm milk
- 100g granulated sugar
- 100g unsalted butter, softened
- 2 large eggs
- 1 teaspoon vanilla extract
- 1/2 teaspoon salt
- 1/2 cup mixed candied fruit (such as citron, orange peel, and lemon peel)
- 1/2 cup golden raisins
- 1/2 cup chopped almonds

For the filling:

- 100g marzipan or almond paste

For the topping:

- Powdered sugar, for dusting

## NUTRITION FACTS:

(per serving, makes about 12 servings)

Calories: 350
Total Fat: 15g
Saturated Fat: 5g
Cholesterol: 45mg
Sodium: 200mg
Total Carbohydrate: 48g
Dietary Fiber: 2g
Sugars: 20g
Protein: 6g

## INSTRUCTIONS:

1. In a large mixing bowl, combine the active sourdough starter, bread flour, lukewarm milk, granulated sugar, softened butter, eggs, vanilla extract, and salt. Mix until a dough forms.

2. Knead the dough for about 10 minutes until smooth and elastic.
3. Fold in the mixed candied fruit, golden raisins, and chopped almonds until evenly distributed throughout the dough.
4. Cover the bowl and let the dough rise at room temperature for 2-3 hours, or until doubled in size.
5. Punch down the dough and roll it out into a large rectangle on a floured surface.
6. Roll out the marzipan or almond paste into a rope slightly shorter than the length of the dough rectangle.
7. Place the marzipan/almond paste rope along one long edge of the dough rectangle.
8. Roll up the dough tightly around the filling, pinching the seam to seal.
9. Shape the rolled dough into a loaf and place it on a parchment-lined baking sheet.
10. Cover the loaf loosely with plastic wrap and let it rise for an additional 1-2 hours, or until puffy.
11. Preheat the oven to 350°F (175°C).
12. Once risen, bake the stollen in the preheated oven for 30-35 minutes, or until golden brown and cooked through.
13. Remove the stollen from the oven and let it cool completely on the baking sheet.
14. Once cooled, dust the top of the stollen with powdered sugar.
15. Slice and serve as desired.

Enjoy your holiday baking with these delicious sourdough recipes! Let me know if you need further assistance or have any questions.

# SOURDOUGH APPLE CIDER DONUTS

**PREP TIME:** 15 minutes | **COOK TIME:** 10-12 minutes | **YIELD:** About 10 donuts

## INGREDIENTS:

- 200g sourdough starter
- 150g all-purpose flour
- 1 teaspoon baking powder
- 1/2 teaspoon baking soda
- 1/2 teaspoon ground cinnamon
- 1/4 teaspoon ground nutmeg
- 1/4 teaspoon salt
- 1/2 cup granulated sugar
- 1/4 cup unsalted butter, melted
- 1/4 cup apple cider
- 1 large egg
- 1 teaspoon vanilla extract

For the coating:

- 1/2 cup granulated sugar
- 1 teaspoon ground cinnamon

## NUTRITION FACTS:

(per serving, makes about 10 donuts)

Calories: 180
Total Fat: 5g
Saturated Fat: 3g
Cholesterol: 30mg
Sodium: 180mg
Total Carbohydrate: 30g
Dietary Fiber: 1g
Sugars: 18g
Protein: 3g

## INSTRUCTIONS:

1. Preheat your oven to 350°F (175°C). Grease a donut pan with butter or non-stick spray.
2. In a mixing bowl, combine the sourdough starter, all-purpose flour, baking powder, baking soda, ground cinnamon, ground nutmeg, and salt. Mix until just combined.
3. In a separate bowl, whisk together the granulated sugar, melted butter, apple cider, egg, and vanilla extract until smooth.
4. Pour the wet ingredients into the dry ingredients and stir until just combined. Be careful not to overmix.

5. Spoon the batter into the prepared donut pan, filling each cavity about 2/3 full.
6. Bake for 10-12 minutes, or until the donuts are lightly golden and spring back when touched.
7. While the donuts are baking, mix together the granulated sugar and ground cinnamon in a shallow bowl to make the coating.
8. Allow the donuts to cool in the pan for a few minutes, then carefully transfer them to a wire rack.
9. While the donuts are still warm, gently roll them in the cinnamon-sugar mixture until coated on all sides.
10. Serve the donuts warm or at room temperature. Enjoy!

These sourdough apple cider donuts are a delightful addition to any holiday spread! Let me know if you need further assistance or have any questions.

# SOURDOUGH HOLIDAY BUCHE DE NOEL (YULE LOG)

**PREP TIME:** 20 minutes (+1 hour chill time)
**COOK TIME:** 10-12 minutes | **YIELD:** About 8 servings

## INGREDIENTS:

For the sponge cake:

- 4 large eggs
- 100g granulated sugar
- 100g all-purpose flour
- 30g cocoa powder
- 1 teaspoon vanilla extract

For the filling:

- 200g sourdough discard
- 250ml heavy cream
- 50g powdered sugar
- 1 teaspoon vanilla extract

For the ganache:

- 150g dark chocolate, chopped
- 150ml heavy cream
- 2 tablespoons unsalted butter

## NUTRITION FACTS:
(per serving, makes about 8 servings)

- Calories: 450
- Total Fat: 30g
- Saturated Fat: 18g
- Cholesterol: 150mg
- Sodium: 80mg
- Total Carbohydrate: 40g
- Dietary Fiber: 2g
- Sugars: 20g
- Protein: 6g

## INSTRUCTIONS:

1. Preheat the oven to 350°F (175°C). Line a 9x13-inch baking sheet with parchment paper.
2. In a large mixing bowl, beat the eggs and granulated sugar until pale and fluffy.

3. Sift in the all-purpose flour and cocoa powder, then gently fold into the egg mixture until well combined.
4. Stir in the vanilla extract.
5. Pour the batter into the prepared baking sheet, spreading it out evenly.
6. Bake for 10-12 minutes, or until the cake springs back when lightly touched.
7. While the cake is baking, prepare the filling by whipping the heavy cream until stiff peaks form. In a separate bowl, mix together the sourdough discard, powdered sugar, and vanilla extract until smooth. Fold the whipped cream into the sourdough mixture until well combined.
8. Once the cake is done baking, remove it from the oven and let it cool slightly.
9. Carefully flip the cake onto a clean kitchen towel dusted with powdered sugar. Peel off the parchment paper.
10. Spread the sourdough filling evenly over the cake.
11. Starting from one short end, gently roll up the cake along with the towel. Place seam-side down on a serving platter.
12. To make the ganache, heat the heavy cream in a small saucepan over medium heat until it begins to simmer. Remove from heat and add the chopped dark chocolate and butter. Let sit for 1-2 minutes, then stir until smooth.
13. Pour the ganache over the rolled cake, spreading it evenly with a spatula to cover the entire surface.
14. Use a fork or knife to create a bark-like texture on the ganache.
15. Chill the Buche de Noel in the refrigerator for at least 1 hour before serving.
16. Optional: Decorate with powdered sugar, cocoa powder, and edible decorations before serving.

www.ingramcontent.com/pod-product-compliance
Lightning Source LLC
Chambersburg PA
CBHW081356130526
44581CB00012B/107